MATILDA MEETS THE UNIVERSE

WRITTEN BY DOM CONLON
ILLUSTRATED BY HEIDI CANNON

uclanpublishing

Praise for
MEET MATILDA ROCKET BUILDER

"A beautiful book full of fun and fascinating
facts which celebrates the joy of embarking on
over-ambitious projects! A must read for all aspiring
rocket scientists, engineers and those who dream big."

Dallas Campbell, TV presenter

"A joyous mix of science, history and story that
will inspire young readers to reach for the stars."

Christopher Edge, author of *Space Oddity*

"The most useful book I have ever read about
building a rocket to take me to the Moon;
maybe this time I'll finally get there. This is a
delightful adventure and inspiration to all
of us who want to be astronauts."

Robin Ince, broadcaster and comedian

For Oliver, who is patiently
teaching me how to think — D.C.

Matilda Meets the Universe is a uclanpublishing book

First published in Great Britain in 2023 by
uclanpublishing
University of Central Lancashire
Preston, PR1 2HE, UK

Text copyright © Dom Conlon, 2023
Illustrations copyright © Heidi Cannon, 2023

978-1-915235-38-1

1 3 5 7 9 10 8 6 4 2

Set in 14/23pt Scribbles AF Felt Tip by Helen Donald, Niamh McBride and Amy Rice.

A CIP catalogue record for this book is available from the British Library.

Printed and bound in Great Britain by Clays Ltd, Elcograf S.p.A.

HAVE YOU EVER WONDERED
HOW BOOKS ARE MADE?

UCLan Publishing is an award-winning independent publisher specialising in Children's and Young Adult books. Based at the University of Central Lancashire, this Preston-based publisher teaches MA Publishing students how to become industry professionals using the content and resources from its business; students are included at every stage of the publishing process and credited for the work that they contribute.

The business doesn't just help publishing students though. UCLan Publishing has supported the employability and real-life work skills for the University's Illustration, Acting, Translation, Animation, Photography, Film & TV students and many more. This is the beauty of books and stories; they fuel many other creative industries! The MA Publishing students are able to get involved from day one with the business and they acquire a behind the scenes experience of what it is like to work for a such a reputable independent.

The MA course was awarded a Times Higher Award (2018) for Innovation in the Arts and the business, UCLan Publishing, was awarded Best Newcomer at the Independent Publishing Guild (2019) for the ethos of teaching publishing using a commercial publishing house. As the business continues to grow, so too does the student experience upon entering this dynamic Masters course.

www.uclanpublishing.com
www.uclanpublishing.com/courses/
uclanpublishing@uclan.ac.uk

Chapter 1

THE MOVIE OF MY AMAZING LIFE

Hi. My name is Matilda Musk. I'm just me and that is enough (Mum would say it's **MORE** than enough). This is my journal and you'd better have asked my permission before reading it.

Everything I learn about myself, my home, my town, my city, my country, my planet, my solar system, my galaxy, my **UNIVERSE**, is written here.

My journal helps me prepare for the big things that will happen in my life. Like, a while back when I tried to build a spaceship, I figured: how difficult can it be? I learned all I could learn until I had the answer:

IT IS VERY DIFFICULT!

But difficult isn't the same as impossible, so I've decided to keep on learning and this time I'm going to prepare myself for something a bit simpler:

MEETING ALIEN LIFE!

That's right. I'm going to be the human who makes first contact.

After this happens, I think aliens and humans will make a film of my life to show how all the things I learned helped bring us all together. That movie will start like this:

On a small* blue** planet in the outer edges of a galaxy . . . Light years from any other planet . . . **8 billion***** people wondered if they were alone . . . But only one girl**** was brave enough to find out.

*   Earth is **40,000 km** around the middle so our small blue planet isn't THAT small. I wouldn't want to walk around it, that's for sure.

**   It's not even completely blue from space, more of a bluey-greeny-brown-white planet.

***   Roughly — but maybe I'm being too picky.

**** ME!

Ok. Now imagine that being said by someone REALLY fabulous — like a superhero or time lord or . . . actually no scratch that, I think I'll be the star of my own film. There will also be some dramatic music and big budget special effects. We'll zoom in from outer space showing a few other planets (just the cool ones) as we go.

Then we'll pass some asteroids, a satellite and maybe a space unicorn before we finally reach EARTH. Then we KEEP zooming in and in and in until finally we see the face of a brave (and determined, and curious, and slightly-cheeky-but-still-lovable) girl who will wink at the camera, plonk a space helmet over her brilliant hair and climb into a spaceship.

Then we'll probably hear Dad shout "MATILDA, DINNER!" and my LITTLE BROTHER'S annoying head will appear in front of the camera where he'll pick his nose and we'll have to carry on tomorrow because I've got homework after tea and then dance practice and I want to go on Discord with Kareem and the others and, well, nobody said making a blockbuster film about the first girl to make contact with alien life would be easy.

That's how the movie of my life will start. But my learning? Well that has to start somewhere too.

I've been learning stuff about the universe for as long as I can remember — which is actually **FOREVER** as far as I'm concerned because I can't ever remember not remembering. I'm like an entire universe!

I think that by the time I leave school more people will have walked on the Moon. And then maybe ten years after that people will have walked on Mars. I could be one of those people. Or I could be working with people as clever as me and I'll have a brilliant brainwave which will help solve a really tricky problem in space exploration. That might sound far-fetched, like what happens in a film, but it isn't. People like me do amazing things all the time — especially when we are working as a team, and especially when that team inspires us and challenges us. It happens in class. I've been listening to a friend talk about her work and suddenly it's given me an idea how I can do my own work. I don't mean in a copycat way, just in a I-can-do-it-too kind of way.

Jerome and Simone are twins in my class and they sometimes finish each other's sentences but they are also really different. Jerome is smart but can be quite annoying and loud whilst Simone is quieter. She says nothing at all for ages and then comes out with something brilliant. I guess they are a kind of team.

I talked to them (and Kareem) a lot when I was trying to build a spaceship and they listened even though spaceships aren't really their thing. But they always made me think a bit harder and be less lazy and more patient. They're my kind of people.

If you're reading this, then I guess you're my kind of people too. Maybe we'll meet one day and talk about space together.

I'd really, really, **REALLY** love to go into space and discover life on another planet. It doesn't have to be a super-intelligent life form (but more intelligent than Dad would be a good start — sorry-not-sorry, Dad). I really don't

fancy meeting a galaxy-conquering, face-eating species or anything. I'd be OK with a quiet sort of species who I can sit and read and eat cheesecake with or something.

But how likely is that?

I don't know. What I do know is that sitting around and doing nothing makes it very **UN**likely. That's why I'm learning all I can about the universe. Like, how did it begin? What's the difference between a planet and a star?

Why does the Moon look as though it changes shape? What else is there in the solar system? What even **IS** a solar system? How far away is the next solar system? How can we

explore other planets? What are the chances of alien life existing? If aliens do exist then how far away might they be and can I catch a bus to visit them?

All this and more will be revealed! I hope my journal makes sense — it's my thoughts, after all and they don't always come out right but I've kept notes about some of the trickiest parts and put those at the back in the **GLOSSARY**.

Right! Let's get on with it.

LIGHTS! CAMERA! ACTION!*

* More like a fairly brief walk to the library.

Chapter 2

WHERE DO I BEGIN?

Picture the scene: my phone rings and I get a call. It's an alien. "Hi, Matilda. I'd like to meet up for a milkshake. Can you meet me at the other end of the universe, please?"

It's the call I've been waiting for but hang on — where is the other end of the universe? How is that different from the other end of the planet, or solar system, or galaxy, or the mess in my room?

Basically . . . what **IS** the universe? If I'm going to find out whether aliens exist and how I'm going to meet them then I need to start right at the beginning. I mean, there's no point looking for snacks in the fridge if I already know that nobody has been to the shops.

I've asked around and done my research and it turns out that the universe is EVERYTHING.

LITERALLY EVERYTHING. As far as we know. And it's around **13.8 billion years old**. I can get a good idea of what's in it just by looking up on a clear night. It's filled with stars — like, **LOADS** of stars.

I know that planets can often be found orbiting stars. Earth orbits our Sun (which is a star) and I know there are other planets close(ish) to Earth. There's Mercury, Venus, Earth, Mars, Saturn, Jupiter, Uranus, and Neptune. There are also other things which are smaller than planets called dwarf planets. Those include Pluto, Eris, Ceres, Makemake, and Haumea. There may be lots more we haven't found yet.

There are also asteroids and comets. I'm going to learn a lot more about everything but the thing I learned first is that the planets and dwarf planets I've mentioned so far are all orbiting our Sun. And the name we have for the area in which everything orbits our Sun is called **THE SOLAR SYSTEM.**

Many stars out there have their own solar systems with planets but there are so many stars that we don't know about all of them.

There might even be lonely stars wandering around looking for planet friends.

The size of a solar system depends on how much mass there is in its star. That's because stars with more mass have a greater gravitational effect than stars with less mass. And the greater that gravitational effect is the wider an area of objects it can cause to orbit it.

Humans have sent spaceships (without people in them) to every planet in our solar system. But it's **SUCH** a long way to the edge of our solar system that only two spaceships have ever left it.

I know I'll need to find out all about that but at the moment I'm just trying to get an idea of what all the stuff that makes up our universe is. And there's way more than just stars, planets and solar systems.

All those systems are also caught in

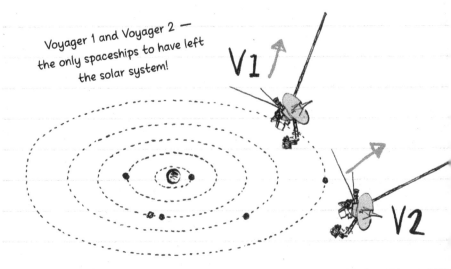

Voyager 1 and Voyager 2 — the only spaceships to have left the solar system!

V1

V2

orbits, only this time they are travelling together in what's called a **GALAXY**.

Galaxies are big. Like, **REALLY** big. And the universe doesn't stop there.

Some galaxies can get together in what's called a local group. Hey! This is sounding a bit like school. Hear me out, it's going to make sense.

We have children who I'm thinking are like the planets. Those children sit around a desk. That's like a solar system. There are lots of desks in a classroom. Think of that as a galaxy.

Then there are groups of classrooms in a school which sounds like a local group to me. I asked Mr Wilson about whether there are groups of schools and he said it depends on what types of schools. There are academies or sometimes they are organised in other ways.

But back to our universe. All these objects and groups eventually get together and, if we zoom out far enough to see **EVERYTHING**, then we call that the universe. Actually, we call it the **OBSERVABLE** universe because there's only so much we can actually see.

That's the other thing to mention: the universe is **MASSIVE**.

That seems obvious, right? Anything which can contain **EVERYTHING** has to be pretty big. That word 'big' doesn't even begin to cover it. Our universe is **93 billion light years** across (46.5 billion light years in every direction). It's been growing for something like **13.8 billion years**. I think I need to really try hard to understand what a light year is and I will but for now I just know that if I hadn't stopped growing for **13.8 billion years** then I'd be pretty big too.

It's not going to be easy to find alien life in such a big universe.

I mean, just think about that size. The edge of our solar system is about **twenty-two billion kilometres** from the Sun. And then it's a long way until the next closest solar system. Solar systems aren't snuggled up next to each other. There's a lot of space in space.

Oh, and there are no signposts.

I need to keep in mind that there are lots of solar systems in a galaxy and lots of galaxies in the (observable) universe. I still need to find out what makes a star a star or a planet a planet, but I know that I can figure it all out with the help of my friends, my teachers, my parents, and the local library (and not my little brother).

But one thing is certain: finding alien life is going to be difficult. Finding out **HOW** difficult is what I'm **ALL** about though so **BRING. IT. ON.**

Chapter 3

BAKING MY OWN UNIVERSE

Another reason why I keep this journal is because I like to get things straight in my head. Learning about space gets so complicated that I find it helps to write things down. I think I understand what sort of things go into making a universe now (stars, planets, asteroids) but I wonder if I'm missing something. I mentioned my problem over dinner one evening and that little brother of mine actually had a good idea: make your own. I didn't tell him it was a good idea, but I started to think about it.

So that's when I made a list of what I'd need if I was going to make a universe.

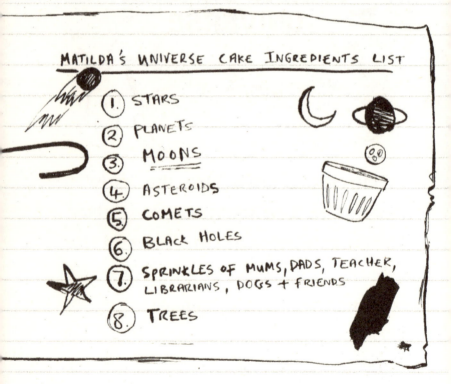

MATILDA'S UNIVERSE CAKE INGREDIENTS LIST

1. STARS
2. PLANETS
3. MOONS
4. ASTEROIDS
5. COMETS
6. BLACK HOLES
7. SPRINKLES OF MUMS, DADS, TEACHER, LIBRARIANS, DOGS + FRIENDS
8. TREES

That sounds easy enough.

The trouble with my list is that it doesn't tell me what stars and planets and mums are made from. There must have been something else before those things.

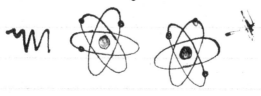

How about atoms? I know that atoms are the building blocks of **EVERYTHING**. When we zoom in on a tree or a stone or a raindrop, we can see that it's made of tiny things called atoms. And what are atoms made from? Well, the smallest, most basic thing there is are things called subatomic particles with names like quarks and gluons. I guess I need to make those first. They'll be like the basic Lego bricks of Matilda's Magnificent Universe! I'll use those to make some really cool aliens which I can meet when I'm older. I'll act really cool and wear sunglasses and say things like

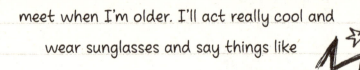

I AM YOUR CREATOR

in a big, booming voice.

Sounds easy enough.

The difficult bit is making those elementary particles stick together to start forming interesting things.

Which is what happened at the Big Bang — or just a fraction of a second after.

I just realised something: I'm kind of rewinding everything to find a starting point — me, planets, stars, atoms, subatomic particles.

This is also how we got to the Big Bang. It's like a detective story, isn't it? Ace Detective, Inspector Matilda sees a crime scene and by clever deduction figures everything out. Case solved.

In **1927** Georges Lemaître did something similar. He noticed that galaxies were moving further apart and realised this was because the universe was **EXPANDING**.

If the universe is expanding, then it makes sense (if I hit the rewind button) that the universe was once smaller. Like if I see a big balloon full of air then I know it was once smaller, with less air in it.

Georges Lemaître worked out that the universe was expanding by looking at the stars and working out whether they were blue shifted or red shifted. **BLUE WHAT?**

Yeah, I didn't know what blue shift or red

shift was either. My top tip for when someone says something you don't understand: **ASK**. Always ask.

When you hear the siren of a fire engine you can tell whether it's headed towards you or away from you. The sound changes.

Sound waves coming towards you get squashed and so make a higher tone than the sound waves moving away from you (which get stretched and make a lower tone). It's like how when we queue up in the playground everyone at the front seems to pack themselves more tightly than the ones at the back who just can't be bothered.

In sound this is called The Doppler Effect. When we talk about light (like the light from the stars) it's called BLUE shift if the light source is moving towards us and RED shift if it's moving away. The star will look redder or bluer depending on the direction and the speed. It's because at one end of the visible light spectrum there is blue and at the other there is red. Blue wavelengths are more squashed than red wavelengths.

Blue wavelengths.

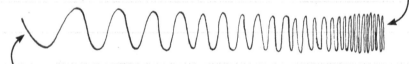

Red wavelengths.

That's how Georges Lemaître noticed that everything was expanding.

Imagine skid marks on a road. They tell us where a car started to skid and where it ended up. We don't need to see the car to understand this.

George measured the amount of red shift, did his sums, hit the big mathematical

REWIND

button and calculated how the universe would have looked a **million**, a **billion** and, finally, **13.8 billion years ago**. That's how long it would have taken to pack all the universe's building blocks so tightly together that you couldn't even fit a sock between them.

When the universe began expanding everything was packed really tightly. That was **13.8 billion years ago**. That isn't the same as saying the universe is **13.8 billion years old**. We don't know HOW old it really is. Just that the Big

Bang occurred that long ago. Nobody knows what happened before that, or how the stuff appeared from nothing (or even **IF** it appeared from nothing). But that's the point when everything interesting began to happen. And it was **SO** tightly packed that not even light could escape.

One instant the universe fitted into a really tiny space, and the next it began getting bigger. Everything needed to build a universe spread out and got to work. And I do mean everything. Stars, planets, cells, the fluff that you get between your toes when you take off your socks, and (hopefully) **ALIENS** — all that was present from the beginning.

Over time (**13.8 billion years**) all those blocks have been rearranged in a **nonillion*** different ways. Nothing ever gets thrown away, it's just reassembled. So you and me are made from the stuff which formed in a star and then shot out into the universe when that star exploded.

I once read that the Big Bang was a super massive **EXPLOSION** which sent stuff flying in all directions.

That isn't what happened.

For starters, it wasn't an explosion — it was an **EXPANSION**.

---

* Nonillion is an actual number — scientists THINK that the highest possible temperature is 142 nonillion Kelvin. That's 142 with 32 zeros after it. I'm pretty sure we'd get sent home from school if that was ever reached. 0 Kelvin is super cold and that is the same as saying -273.15 degrees Celsius. So 142 nonillion Kelvin is a completely bonkers temperature but that's how hot the entire universe was at the start of EVERYTHING.

An explosion suggests stuff erupting into something else, like smoke filling a room. But I need to think of the Big Bang as the smoke AND the room. They both began expanding and spreading out.

This part of the Big Bang is called **INFLATION**.

Inflation was a very sudden, very brief, very **HUGE** expansion. The universe went from one size to a **MUCH** larger size in way less than a second. Like when you look around to check the coast is clear and then start telling your best friend (Kareem) how you once saw your grandma pick her nose and then **BOOM** — Kareem's eyes widen and you realise Grandma has just appeared **MASSIVELY** right behind you.

Let's never talk about this again.

The point is, everything unpacked and from that came everything else. Inflation gave it a boost but then the expansion rate settled down. It took a whopping **380,000 years** for the universe to become cool enough and spread out enough for light to start shining and atoms to start forming. That's a great start (or an "encouraging beginning" as one teacher-who-shall-remain-nameless once scribbled on a story I'd written) but it took **200 million years** for the first stars to be born.

So how do the aliens come into this? Well, if the stuff you, me, Earth, cheese, and stars are made from all came out of that Big Bang then I think there's plenty of stuff to make aliens. The question is: what are the chances of that? My thinking is that it's a pretty big universe so maybe there's a good chance.

Hang on though: how big is **BIG**?

Chapter 4

YOU GO ON AND ON AND ON AND ON AND . . .

Phew. That was heavy going! All I want to know is everything — is that too much to ask?

The Big Bang happened **13.8 billion years ago** and everything has been expanding ever since. So how far has it expanded?

I've been wondering about this for ages, way before I could pop to a library or look it up online. I once asked Dad how big the universe was but all he said was "how long is a piece of string". I measured a piece of string and it was **11.8cm**. I know for a fact that the universe is not **11.8cm** long.

The word which usually pops up when I ask about this is: **INFINITE**. The universe is infinite. Which I understand as **FOREVER. WITHOUT END. ON AND ON.** And all the things you'd put in **CAPITAL LETTERS** to show how **BIG** the concept is.

But what does that mean? What is infinite?

Think of a number between **6** and **7**.

Stuck?

Maybe you were smart and thought about **6.5** or something. You could keep adding numbers. Like **6.5537182737363 78292929** and on and on and on and on **FOREVER**. There are **INFINITE** numbers between **6** and **7**.

You can do the same thing when measuring distance.

I asked Dad if we could conduct an experiment. I filled a paper plate with custard and then explained that in order for the plate to reach his face it would need to travel half the distance between me and him. After that it would need to travel the other half.

But I can also divide the second half into two halves.

First it covers the first half, then the second.

I can keep dividing that second half **FOREVER**. It will **ALWAYS** need to cover half the remaining distance even though that half will keep getting smaller and smaller.

So how can it **EVER** reach my Dad's face if it keeps having to travel across these smaller and smaller halves? This is something called Zeno's Paradox. **ZENO** was not, as I first thought, a dastardly space villain in a cartoon, but a philosopher from **two and a half thousand years ago.**

According to my maths, the plate should have been trapped **FOREVER** covering half the remaining distance (and half the remaining remaining distance and so on).

It didn't.

Dad was NOT happy and would like a word with Zeno.

MAW-HA-HA!!

The upside is that I learned that the idea of **INFINITE** is a pretty strange thing. There are **LOADS** of different types of **INFINITE** and measuring the universe includes one of them.

When people talk about the size of the universe they are usually talking about the **OBSERVABLE** universe. But what's the observable universe and how do we measure it? It's the bit we can see (and ever hope to see) even with the biggest telescope **EVER**. To understand why we first have to accept that **SEEING** involves **LIGHT** travelling from an object to our eyes.

That's because light doesn't move from an object to our eyes in an instant.

It takes time.

It's still **REALLY** fast (**299,792.458 kilometres per second**) but when something is far away, those seconds start adding up.

In one second a photon of light will circle the Earth about **seven and a half times**. That's fast!

But it takes **eight and a half minutes** for it to travel from the Sun to Earth. Which shows just how far away the Sun is.

So really, when you see anything, you see how it was when light first left it or bounced off it.

I didn't know this until Mr Wilson talked about the dinosaurs in Year 5.

DINOSAURS!

What on EARTH do dinosaurs have to do with the light we see?

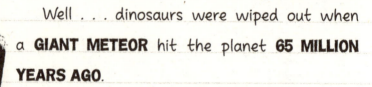

Well . . . dinosaurs were wiped out when a **GIANT METEOR** hit the planet **65 MILLION YEARS AGO**.

There's a galaxy called **NGC 4845** which is **65 million LIGHT YEARS** away from Earth. When things get REALLY far away we start measuring it in light years — the distance light travels in a year (**9.46 TRILLION kilometres**). It makes sense to call such massive distances light years for the same reason it makes sense to call ten millimetres "one centimetre", one hundred centimetres "one metre", and so on. If I run for **5 km** (hahaha — unlikely) then I don't want to say I've done a **5,000,000 mm** sprint (more like stagger). It's the same when we are talking about **TRILLIONS** of kilometres. It's just so much easier to say **LIGHT YEARS**. Plus it sounds way cooler.

Mr Wilson told us that when we look at

NGC 4845 in the night sky we are seeing light which left it at the time when the dinosaurs became extinct (kaput, deceased, no more). So really when we are looking at the stars we are looking into the past. Some of the stars we see might have died a long time ago.

Flip that around and if someone was standing on a planet in NGC 4845 right NOW looking at Earth through a telescope, they would see the extinction of the dinosaurs. Or rather, they'd see the light reflecting off Earth which left at that time — it would need to be a SUPER powerful telescope to see actual dinosaurs.

It's the same with everything. It takes time for the light to bounce off your face and hit my eyes. It's only a tiny tiny **TEENY** amount of time but we are only ever looking at the past.

So that's how we examine what the universe looked like **BILLIONS** of years ago. It's also why when we say 'universe' we mostly mean 'the observable universe'. We can only see the part of the universe where light has had time to reach us.

Even if we could travel at the **SPEED OF LIGHT** (which is the fastest speed possible) we would never be able to reach the edge of the universe (if there even is one) because not only is the universe **STILL** expanding, it's had a **13.8 billion year** head start.

Once I'd learned all this, I tried my best to teach Dad because I thought his 'how long is a piece of string' answer was a bit rubbish. He said he'd changed his mind and that it was **93 billion light years**, plus a bit extra in the time I'd been talking to him.

It's a bit bigger now.

And now.

And . . . OK, DAD — I GET IT!

The problem with asking Dad is that he doesn't always explain WHY something is the way it is. I had to do more research to find out WHY the **OBSERVABLE** universe is **93 billion light years** across. Because, if you think about it, if light speed is the fastest speed there is and the universe has been expanding for **13.8 billion years** then SURELY it should only be **27.6 billion light years** across (**13.8 billion light years** in one direction and **13.8 billion light years** in the other — with ME at the centre).

The BIG, BONKERS thing to try and

understand is that every part of the universe is STILL expanding. It's not just the edges.

That's why for this example I'll think of the universe as a partially inflated balloon. When it gets bigger, it ALL gets bigger.

So OK, let's talk about how the universe expands.

The universe is a balloon, right? If I set an ant walking along its surface then it might walk **two centimetres** in a **second**. If I inflate the balloon whilst the ant is walking then the ant will travel further even though it's going at the same speed for the same amount of time. That's because the surface is expanding.

So that means light (or the ant in my example) is travelling at the same speed but the distance it covers is greater than it would be if the universe wasn't expanding.

I did try to do this as an experiment, but ants are really unhelpful. When it comes to making the movie of my life then I think we'll need some special effects. Or well-trained ants.

But here's something else for my journal: that word **OBSERVABLE**.

I used to think all this observation was done through a massive telescope — one of those you stuck your eye too and then went OOOH and AAAH as you see the moons of Jupiter or the fuzzy nebula on Orion's Sword. But hold on to your sunglasses because . . .

WE DON'T ALWAYS USE OUR EYES TO SEE THE UNIVERSE.

Visible light is just one part of how we see the universe. As well as the colours we all see and sing about (I can sing a rainbow, sing a rainbow) there is infrared light and ultraviolet light. And it doesn't stop there. There are x-rays, gamma rays, microwaves (PING . . . your universe is now cooked) and radio waves.

All of these exist on **THE ELECTROMAGNETIC SPECTRUM** and I think I've got a LOT more learning to do.

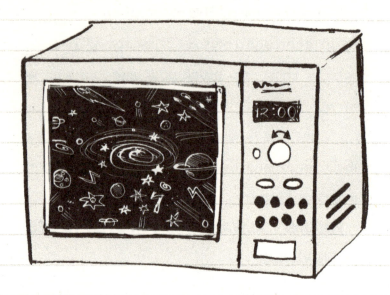

Chapter 5

LOOK OUT!

What goes BEEP BEEP BEEP BEEP and looks like a potato?

SPUD-NIK 1.

You're not laughing.

OK, so that wasn't my best joke. I told Mum that joke and she handed me a bag of potatoes and told me to start peeling. Being a science whizz doesn't get you out of making dinner.

In **1957**, the Soviet Union launched the VERY first artificial satellite. The Soviet Union was a collection of countries grouped together under one label (a bit like the United Kingdom). It no longer exists in the same way but one of the countries, Russia, still does a lot of space missions.

That first satellite was called Sputnik 1 and it talked to people on Earth by sending out a radio signal ("beep beep beep" rather than "hello, you're listening to Radio Matilda and we have a caller on the line").

Radio waves, as I said before, are a part of the **ELECTROMAGNETIC SPECTRUM** and they contain **INFORMATION**. And just like visible light, radio waves also travel at the speed of light. Radio waves have also been travelling since the Big Bang bonged its gong which means we can listen carefully and decode that information.

In fact, the entire (wait for it) **ELECTROMAGNETIC SPECTRUM** can give us important information about the universe.

And oh boy, do we need it.

You see, the trouble with looking for light from the start of the universe is that we can't see it. Imagine that! Light you can't see. Everything was too tightly packed together for anything to travel very far and the universe was opaque. In order to look back to the VERY beginning, scientists have to examine what's left over — which is like understanding what I had for my tea by looking at the chips which had black bits in, and the tomato sauce on my plate*.

That's where the entire spectrum comes in.

There are bits of the electromagnetic

---

* OK, my jumper.

spectrum that we can see with our eyes (colours) which are really useful in measuring the movement of stars.

The red shift and blue shift stuff happens when an object moves away from us or towards us. I've already written about how important that is in helping us see that the universe is expanding.

But all the other parts of the spectrum are important too. They can give us information about what stars are made of, what space looks like, and even what the universe looked like when it was very very young (about **380,000 years old** — poor baby). Looking at the ultraviolet or infrared light given off by a star will tell us different things than the regular visible (to our eyes) light.

The energy given off as microwaves in the early stages of the universe left an imprint which can be detected today by powerful radio telescopes. The imprint is a kind of map, showing us where the highest areas of energy were.

It's called the cosmic microwave background radiation.

EMBARRASSING CONFESSION TIME!

This wasn't me but SOMEONE I KNOW once stood up after sitting on a sofa on a VERY WARM day. On the seat was a VERY SWEATY BUM PRINT.

That's the cosmic microwave background radiation.

Kind of.

Not really.

Sort of.

When the universe was super hot, atoms couldn't form. There were photons and electrons (the smaller bits of atoms) but they couldn't stick together (which is weird because

when it's hot I seem to stick to everything).
That left the photons just bouncing around like
light on a foggy day. Once the universe started
to cool, all that radiation was released, and
it left a heat map which shows the regions
where galaxies began to form (in the hotter,
denser parts).

It's the biggest sweaty bum print ever!

All this is really very cool (or very very hot)
but that map isn't the sort that comes with a
big arrow saying "**ALIENS LIVE HERE**".

I just want to know where they might live.
Is that too much to ask?

I sat Mum and Dad down to go through
everything I've learned so far. I was thinking
maybe they might see something I couldn't.

They didn't.

Mum just said I should have my own radio
show so I can . . . hang on . . .

I just had an idea.

An idea so amazing I think I can feel it becoming part of the cosmic microwave background.

I wonder if I can use the electromagnetic spectrum to hunt for aliens? Or at least part of it.

The radio wave part.

Chapter 6

LISTEN UP!

Kareem called over today. He usually sends me a message first, but he'd left his phone at home. The first I knew of his visit was when I saw his face pressed against the front window. Mum was knitting a jumper for the tortoise and Dad was counting the arms and legs of my little brother because he was convinced that he'd been replaced by an alien. We all leapt to our feet and shouted because Kareem looked like a hideous monster.

He'd been out collecting seaweed and had it draped all over him. He thought we might like to eat it for tea, but we went to the chippy instead.

Why am I telling you this?

Because, whilst I'm not ENTIRELY convinced that Kareem isn't some kind of weird time-travelling alien, he interrupted me when I was reading about **SETI**.

It turns out that I'm not the only one searching for aliens.

SETI stands for the **S**earch for **E**xtra**t**errestrial **I**ntelligence. Extraterrestrial is another word for **ALIEN**, and **ALIEN** is another word for life forms other than ourselves. The thing is, I've heard the word aliens used for humans too, which makes me think we (humans) have a bit of a problem accepting other forms of life into our family, so I like the word 'extraterrestrial' because that is a way of saying 'life on planets which aren't Earth'. Terra means land, or earth. We get the words 'terrain', 'territory' and 'Terry's chocolate orange'* from that.

SETI is an organisation which looks for signs of intelligent life on other planets and it does this by listening to the universe.

BEEP BEEP BEEP BEEP.

That radio wave part of the **ELECTROMAGNETIC SPECTRUM** turns out to be really interesting and really useful.

The entire electromagnetic spectrum is made up of naturally occurring waves of radiation. The radio part of it is just a range of that spectrum, made up of certain wavelengths

* I made that up because I'm eating one right now.

This is the radio part of the electromagnetic spectrum:

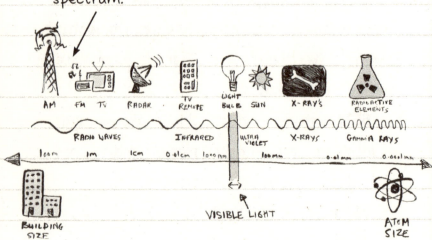

AM FM TV RADAR TV REMOTE LIGHT BULB SUN X-RAY'S RADIOACTIVE ELEMENTS

RADIO WAVES   INFRARED   ULTRA VIOLET   X-RAYS   GAMMA RAYS

100m   1m   1cm   0.01cm 1000 mm   100 mm   0.01 mm   0.0001 mm

VISIBLE LIGHT

BUILDING SIZE

ATOM SIZE

In **1865** James Clerk Maxwell proved the existence of electromagnetic waves which travel at the speed of light. His work led to the invention of . . . you guessed it . . . **RADIO**.

Great-Grandad calls the radio a WIRELESS. Plug the wireless in, Matilda, he says and I say WHOA, GRAMPS — I thought you said it was wireless! He tells me not to sass him.

I mostly listen to podcasts which are streamed over the internet but we have an old radio in the kitchen. You turn the dial and tune it into different frequencies (wavelengths) to get different shows. It's a bit of an effort when I can just shout "ALEXA, PLAY THOSE FUNKY SPACE TUNES".

The thing about radio waves is that ever since we started broadcasting them, they've been leaking out into space.

Maybe aliens living on a planet **100 light years** away are listening to the early broadcasts which people on Earth made, in the same way as the extraterrestrials on a planet in the **NGC 4845** galaxy are watching the meteor wipe out all our dinosaurs.

When Kareem turned up looking like a creature from an alien swamp, I had just read how **SETI** were listening to all the radio frequencies in the hope of hearing some FUNKY SPACE TUNES by alien singers like Bruno Mars.

SETI uses radio telescopes to listen, but anyone can hear radio waves from space.

Kareem and I took the radio up to my room and turned the dial. We went through channels of music and people talking (regular, Earth people — not extraterrestrials), but sometimes we heard a hissing noise. This noise is called static and some of it comes from space. It's all mixed in with noise from the million other things down here on Earth which emit radio waves though, so we gave up trying to pick out anything useful.

SETI uses better radio receivers than our old kitchen one but even they haven't found anything yet. There's a LOT of noise out there but there's also another problem — radio waves aren't only sent out by people (whatever planet they live on). And another problem is that whilst radio waves travel at the speed of light, they still take time to reach Earth. That means if someone is standing on a planet in NGC 4845 (remember that galaxy?) trying to detect our radio signals then they'd need to start listening **65 million years** from now, because that's how long it would take our signal to reach their planet if we started broadcasting now.

That's not the only issue.

Radios and mobile phones send out radio waves. But so does almost every object in the universe, including stars. Figuring out what those objects are can be quite tricky.

Luckily there's one object which sends out really helpful radio signals. That object is a type of star called a **PULSAR**.

Pulsars were first identified by Jocelyn Bell Burnell, and they are super important because they help us search for planets beyond our solar system. A pulsar is a star which ran out of fuel and collapsed into a really dense, small object called a neutron star. When that happened, all its starry gas was flung off into space (that's called a supernova and I think I need to learn a bit more about that because they sound AWESOME). The pulsar has all the mass of a bigger star than our own but is only about the size of a city. I imagine it would be like when I crush an empty can into something much more solid.

The pulsar acts like a kind of cosmic clock because it spins and sends out a beam of light at very regular intervals. We pick up this beam as a radio signal. And whenever it stops being reliable then we know SOMETHING IS GOING ON. It might be that something is blocking the signal every now and again. And that something could be a planet! It's certainly worth listening more closely to detect the pattern of the blocking.

I've been scribbling a lot of stuff about stars and planets, but I didn't always know the difference between them. It's important to get this right because if I'm going to find alien life then I need to look in the right place.

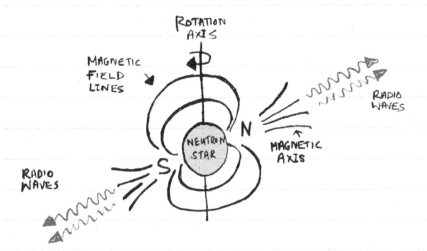

Chapter 7

PLANETS WITH STAR POWER

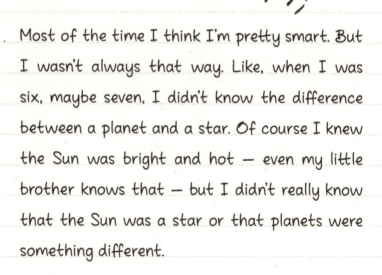

Most of the time I think I'm pretty smart. But I wasn't always that way. Like, when I was six, maybe seven, I didn't know the difference between a planet and a star. Of course I knew the Sun was bright and hot — even my little brother knows that — but I didn't really know that the Sun was a star or that planets were something different.

I needed to up my learning game a bit. For some reason I decided to ask Dad.

He told me that the answer is long and complicated but then Mum walked past and said that a star is a burning ball of gas, and a planet is a big lump of rock.

Dad muttered something about simple answers for simple people and I snatched the brownie he was about to tuck into, gave him a smile and told them both I was off to the Moon.

If only I'd managed to get away quicker. I love learning but Dad has a way of teaching which takes **FOREVER** (I can feel the universe expanding as he talks). And I know one of his lectures is coming because he calls me '**VALENTILDA**'.

He calls me that because Valentina Tereshkova was the first woman in space, and he wants to inspire me. He also calls me a weird alien, so I wouldn't really recommend listening to him.

Mum tried to make a speedy exit too, only she chose to put a lead on our tortoise and take him for a walk. One day I need to have a talk with her about **HOW TO MAKE A QUICK GETAWAY**.

At least I had a brownie to eat though. I could munch through one of those whilst he lectured me.

Only . . . I couldn't.

The brownie was about **2cm** away from a rendezvous with my tummy (Buzz Aldrin would be proud of me) when Dad whipped it out of my hand and placed it on the table.

OK, I need to warn all you younger readers now. What follows is upsetting. Deeply upsetting. You can skip ahead to the next chapter if you'd like. I would.

Still here? You're brave. Or stupid.

What happened next was that Dad **SMASHED** the brownie. That's right. **DESTROYED IT**. He got his fingers right into it and broke it into **CRUMBS**.

My heart sank. And so did my tummy.

The smashed brownie was supposed to represent the early solar system.

He told me to imagine back to a time **FOUR AND A HALF BILLION YEARS AGO**, before our Sun formed.

That brownie would totally be out of date by now. But yeah, I'd still eat it.

Then he made wavy movements with his hands. I've seen adults do this. It's supposed to be a funny way of showing we are thinking back in time. It isn't funny.

So back in the early solar system there was a lot of dust and a lot of gas. Not the kind of gas my little brother seems to specialise in though.

Mum was still doing her best to take the tortoise for a walk but I'm going to save you the (what felt like) twelve hours of DAD TALKING to give you the cheat notes on it. He did make sense but NEVER EVER tell him I said that.

The force of gravity means everything is attracted to everything else. Which, in the case of our Sun forming, means the dust and gas began to be pulled towards one another like an EVIL ROBOT ASSEMBLING ITSELF. Because the particles of gas and dust were so tiny this was very slow to start with, but small bits became larger bits which meant the influence of gravity was stronger and could reach further.

Anyway, when things collide, they get hotter. Just try clapping your hands and you can test that.

The more the gas clumped together the hotter it became. And when it grew quite large it grew very hot and all that heat caused all that dust to twirl around the gas and then. . .

WOOF! IT IGNITED!

The big ball of plasma became a protostar which became hotter and hotter, squeezing more and more of the gas together until it was a huge ball of burning gas which we call ... **THE SUN**.

That was pretty much (as far as I could see) exactly what Mum had said in one sentence.

I was listening to him but to be honest, I was mostly staring sadly at the brownie crumbs. He began to push them together. You see, big as it was, the Sun didn't use up ALL the gas and dust — only about **99%** of it (which sounds a lot — actually, it is a LOT).

The rest of the dust became the planets. There wasn't enough to make an object large enough to form another star but we managed to get eight pretty nice planets out of it. And some dwarf planets (like Pluto).

Four of the planets (Mercury, Venus, Earth, and Mars) were rocky and the larger planets were big enough to do something pretty terrific. They became **GAS GIANTS**.

We call those Jupiter, Saturn, Uranus, and Neptune.

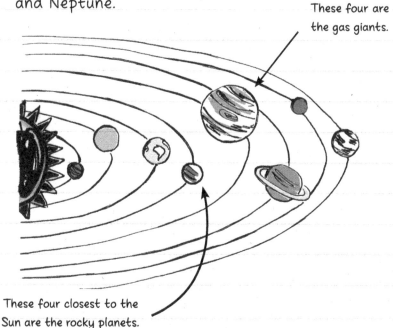

These four are the gas giants.

These four closest to the Sun are the rocky planets.

So Mum wasn't quite right when she said planets were rocky. Some are, some aren't.

All this took a very long time — millions and millions of years — but I think it was still quicker than listening to Dad, or watching Mum take the tortoise for a walk.

So that's the difference between a planet and a star. The star is so hot that it gobbles up its fuel (all the stuff it's made from), but in doing so it creates two really amazing things: **HEAT** and **LIGHT**. Both of which make life on planets possible. Or some planets, anyway. Well . . . actually . . . just one, so far as we know. **AT THE MOMENT**.

Of course, you are probably wondering about the **BIGGEST QUESTION OF THEM ALL**.

What happened to the

brownie after Dad fudged it all together into a big chocolatey star (with what looked like some pencil shavings and at least one fingernail clipping)?

HE ATE IT.

"It's all energy," he said, and popped it into the great black hole he calls a mouth.

Once I learned what a star was, I knew that I could at least tick those off my list of places to look for extraterrestrial life.

Or could I?

Chapter 8

NOW I'M SEEING THINGS

OK — just so we're clear: star = big ball of burning gas; planet = big ball of rock, ice, or gas which isn't burning.

That seems pretty simple.

So why oh WHY did people once think life could exist ON A STAR? It's like thinking something could be living inside our oven.

Oops. I just said that bit out loud as I was writing and Dad is now wearing yellow

gloves and shouting "COME OUT" with his head in the oven.

But it's true, people did once think life could survive on the Sun.

It's not as daft as it seems though.

I caught Grandad shouting across the road at a tree. "Clear off!" he yelled. "I know your parents," he warned.

When I asked him why he was shouting at a tree he squinted then dug out his glasses and looked again. "I'll let you off this time," he muttered, and went back into the house.

I wasn't surprised. He keeps telling everyone he doesn't really need to wear glasses and then mistakes a bin or tree for people he knows. He once mistook me for a post-box and I'd eaten half his letter by the time he realised.

People have been doing the same thing about aliens for as long as we've thought there ARE such a thing as aliens.

It's all because of **SUNSPOTS**. So that's something ELSE I'm going to have to learn about. How does the Sun get SPOTS? By not washing her face. You'd better be sure to clean your face twice a day, Ms Sunshine.

Oh. It turns out that the Sun doesn't get THOSE kind of spots.

The Sun is a mess. It's like a beautiful, angry redhead (like my friends the twins, Jerome and Simone). Only that isn't hair on the Sun, it's plasma and magnetic fields.

I opened my magnet set yesterday and scattered iron filings on paper over one of the biggest magnets. It formed a pattern of lines which swept up and around like big hoops connecting north to south.

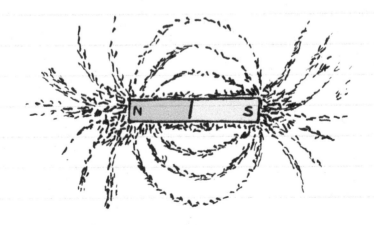

That's how I thought all
magnets work. The Earth has
a magnetic field which looks
like that (if you had a piece
of paper big enough). There's a
north at one end and a south at
the other.

The Sun does things differently.
For a start, it rotates differently.
Earth rotates on its axis once a day. But that
rotation doesn't jiggle all the countries up.
So Greenland doesn't end up in a different spot
in relation to Antigua each day. The Sun, however,
isn't a solid ball of rock so parts of it rotate
at different speeds to other parts. It's like
a Rubik's sphere except it only has horizontal
sections.

That sounds kinda twisty and looks more
like this:

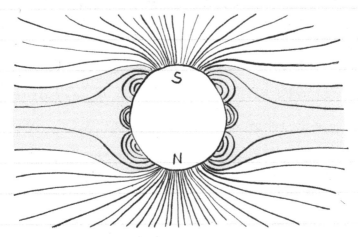

And it also sounds kinda like what happened when my little brother used to get his nappy in a twist whilst trying to get out of it.

Eventually all those twists become a bit too much and **SPROING** . . . it suddenly untwists with a whole load of energy.

When that happens to the Sun, the result is that massive solar flares leap out like fiery whips. They send solar energy out into space.

When it happened with my little brother . . . well . . . I don't want to talk about THAT.

Those solar flares can seriously affect life on Earth. They can interfere with radios and make the aurora (the lights in the sky seen towards the North and South Poles*) even more amazing.

But what does all that have to do with sunspots and aliens living on the Sun?

The crazy turmoil of the magnetic field means that it's stronger in some parts of the Sun than in other parts. When the south and north poles of a magnet push away from each other they create an area between the poles. On the Sun's surface these forces keep some of the heat away and these cooler areas appear darker.

SUNSPOTS!

Even though they are cooler, they are still VERY hot — over **3,500 degrees Celsius**!

Those spots can get **PRETTY BIG**. Not just

---

* The lights are called 'aurora borealis' in the north, and 'aurora australis' in the south.

BIG but **PLANET BIG**. And not just **EARTH PLANET BIG** but **JUPITER PLANET BIG**. Which means people on Earth have been able to SPOT them (hahaha) for hundreds of years even with the most basic of solar telescopes.

But just like my Grandad thinking a post box was a person, some people began to think that those spots might be caves. And if there were caves in the Sun then maybe they were cool enough to contain life.

In **1781**, Sir William Herschel found a new planet in our solar system. He called it the Georgian Star but everyone said "shush, that's a rubbish name" *. Now we call that planet 'Uranus'.

Herschel was a bit of a whizz (just like me) with telescopes and really helped push science

---

* They might NOT have actually said that, but it is a rubbish name.

This is the telescope William Herschel made! It was 40 feet (over 12 metres) tall!

forward. He made the term 'asteroid' popular with other scientists. He also studied sunspots. But even he had to guess at some things and one of his guesses was that the Sun might have people living inside it.

But that's not a daft thing to do. Loads of things come from people making a guess first and then testing the guess. Sometimes it works out and sometimes it doesn't. I like to make wild guesses about cakes and then test my theories by eating them. One day I'll write a scientific paper on the subject.

I've looked at old drawings made of the Moon when telescopes were new and we were just beginning to learn some of the secrets of the universe. The dark bits look like seas which is why they were given the name **MARE** (which means 'sea' in Latin and is pronounced 'MAH-RAY'). If people thought that the Moon had seas on it (it never did but they didn't know that back then) then it's also not daft to think there would be life there. People weren't stupid in the olden days; they just did the best with the facts and technology they had. We still do.

All this has got me thinking about the Moon. Last year I tried to build my own spaceship and learned a lot about it, but I had to start with a much simpler question: why does the Moon change shape?

Chapter 9

WHO ATE THE <u>MOON</u>?

I still plan on going to the Moon someday. That's why I'm keeping notes in this journal. I'm sure they will probably get put behind glass in a big museum for children to look at and go: "Oh wow, that's actual writing from the greatest space adventurer ever." And then a dusty museum person will tell them to shush and not get their greasy fingers on the glass.

But I'm getting ahead of myself.

When I was five, I asked Dad why the Moon changed shape. He was making an egg and cheese sandwich at the time, which always takes him **AGES**. It's like he's constructing a work of art or something. Anyway, he said "Ask your Mum", and went off in search of pickles.

I asked Mum and she turned the question back on me, **LIKE SHE ALWAYS DOES**, and asked why I thought the Moon changed shape. Like she couldn't just TELL me.

Top tip for any of you who get a response like this: go big or go home. And by that I mean just think of answers so completely bonkers that the adult in your life will have no choice but to get to the point and give you the answer*.

I looked at Dad's sandwich and said "A giant space mouse eats it."

Confession time: I was five years old, remember. I may have actually really properly believed that a giant space mouse was responsible for eating the Moon.

* Note: this doesn't seem to work on teachers.

Now the thing about science is that it often comes from people having an idea and then testing to see if it's right or wrong. I've said this before and every time I have an idea, I ask myself "Can I test that idea?"

I now know that my giant space mouse idea is wrong not because it was a silly idea but because I can test it by observing the Moon very carefully to see if it ever gets eaten by a giant space mouse.

The answer (if you are wondering) is that it doesn't. I know this after I sat watching the Moon through my telescope.

But that doesn't help me understand why the Moon does change shape.

Mum helped though. And she helped by setting up an experiment where we could test what was happening.

She grabbed the iPad (which Dad was using

as a plate) and showed me some pictures of the Moon going from full and bright to a circle of black.

To be honest, it did look like something had been nibbling it.

Mum gave me her 'I'm-not-saying-anything-because-this-is-an-important-lesson' look and I shut up.

She tapped the screen and showed me some more pictures. Only this time the Moon was changing in the opposite way. It started as a circle of black and ended as a full, bright Moon. That was a problem. If it was being nibbled then it couldn't go from black to bright again.

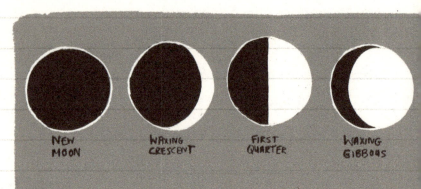

NEW MOON   WAXING CRESCENT   FIRST QUARTER   WAXING GIBBOUS

I wanted-to-maybe-actually-DID-say "MOUSE VOMIT", but we won't dwell on that.

A five-year-old's brain is a brilliant thing though and I began to think about what the Moon was made from.

I really wanted to say cheese. But I knew it was rock.

There goes my giant space mouse theory.

The room was as quiet as . . . as . . . oh I can't think of a good simile. Anyway, it was quiet. Even my deeply annoying little brother was quiet. And, miracle of miracles, Dad had put down his egg, Nutella and pickle sandwich in order to listen. Dads can't do two things

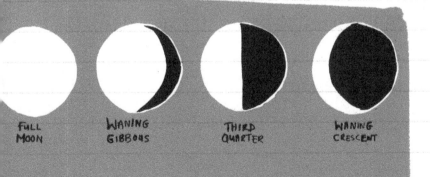

FULL MOON   WANING GIBBOUS   THIRD QUARTER   WANING CRESCENT

at once. Though, to be fair, he was also managing to keep an eye on the sandwich.

Mum explained that the Moon goes around the Earth and that the word for that is 'orbit'.

I like that word.

I began to orbit Dad's sandwich and managed to block Dad's view. He panicked but Mum clapped her hands as though I was the cleverest five-year-old on this or any other planet.

See, this is kind of what happens with the Moon.

Mum told me to get a torch and turn out the lights which I did, but then Dad tripped over my baby brother and we had to wait until he was asleep again.

The torch, in this mad family experiment,

was the Sun. Dad objected to this because he thought the Moon only came out at night.

Facepalm! Even back then I knew the Sun didn't get switched off at night and I'd even seen the Moon during the day, so I climbed on a chair and patted him on the head. It's not nice to make other people feel stupid but I felt it would be fine with Dad.

I got to play the role of Earth. Oh, the power!

Mum got to be the Moon. Dad became the Sun by holding the torch. Somehow the Sun didn't seem so amazing any more.

Then Mum stood facing me but with her back to Dad. She was all dark. This is called a New Moon. None of the Sun's light is reflecting on the side of the Moon I could see.

My nibble theory was based on going from a Full Moon (which is big and bright) to the New Moon which you can't actually see in the sky. But it turns out that it's better to see the phases of the Moon as going from New to Full and then back to New.

I was beginning to see where this was going.

Then Mum began to move around . . . sorry . . . **ORBIT** . . . me.

She moved anti-clockwise to my left. If I was a clock, she would be between **ten** and **eleven**. The light now caught only a bit of her face in a crescent-shaped glow on the right-hand side.

The Moon in this part of the phase is called a Crescent Moon and it's **WAXING**. That means it's getting bigger.

She moved again and stood at nine o'clock. I could see the light/shadow was half and half. That's called the first quarter even though it looks half full.

These days I think of the phases as quarters of the roughly **twenty-seven days** it takes to go right around Earth.

Mum carried on orbiting my head and the light became fatter. When it's more than half then it's called **GIBBOUS**. It's still getting bigger so it's still waxing.

I had to turn my body to see her of course — I'm not some kind of weird human owl thing.

By this point she was standing on the other side of me, opposite Dad. She's taller than me (obviously) so her face was lit up entirely. I knew this one. It's a **FULL MOON**.

Dad was bored of being the Sun.

Honestly, my brother has a better attention span than he does.

I understood exactly what the phases of the Moon were now, but you know adults, once they start they just can't stop. Mum carried on with her orbit.

As she walked further around, the light became thinner but still took up more than half her face.

She was a **GIBBON**! Sorry, a **GIBBOUS** Moon.

When the Moon is going from Full to New it's called **WANING**.

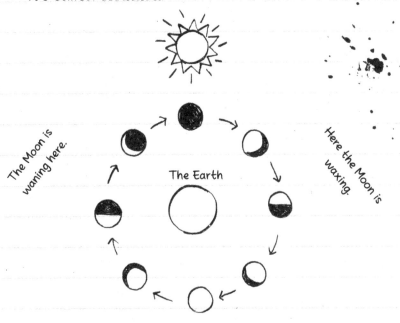

The Moon is waning here.

The Earth

Here the Moon is waxing.

I remembered this because there was a boy in school who was called Wayne. He was always complaining about being too hot, too cold, too hungry, not hungry enough. You name it, he complained about it. Miss Dough told him to stop whining and so afterwards we always told him to stop wayning.

When Mum's face was half in light (the left side this time) and half in shadow she was 'third quarter'.

Dad and I watched as the light grew thinner, back into a crescent shape, and then to where she'd started off with her back to Dad. That's called a New Moon.

Understanding the phases of the Moon is a lot easier than I'd thought (though still not as exciting as a giant space mouse). I could see why eating bits of the Moon wouldn't work though because nobody was going to be building an exact replica of it every **twenty-seven days**.

Moons are definitely amazing though. The one we see in our sky isn't the only one in our solar system. Along with the planets there are **LOADS** of moons. Mercury and Venus don't have any, but Mars has two, Jupiter has ninety-two (but only fifty-three of them have names at the moment). Saturn has even more — at least eighty-three (fifty-three we are sure about and twenty-nine we're still wondering about). Uranus has twenty-seven moons and Neptune has fourteen. And of course, let's **NEVER** forget our own lovely Moon.

That's a lot of moons! Maybe I could visit them all one day.

So that's how I finally learned about the phases of the Moon. Dad learned something else too because  when he put the big lights on, he discovered that his sandwich was missing.

All I will say on this matter is that scientifically speaking, egg, Nutella and pickle do not taste nice together.

Chapter 10

GOLDILOCKS AND THE SEVEN BEARS

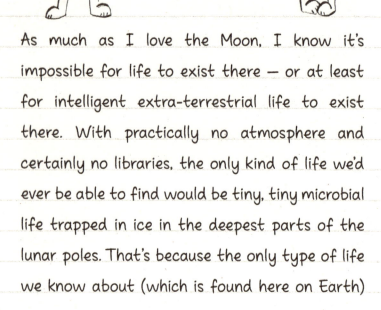

As much as I love the Moon, I know it's impossible for life to exist there — or at least for intelligent extra-terrestrial life to exist there. With practically no atmosphere and certainly no libraries, the only kind of life we'd ever be able to find would be tiny, tiny microbial life trapped in ice in the deepest parts of the lunar poles. That's because the only type of life we know about (which is found here on Earth)

is made up of stuff not found in the right sort of conditions on the Moon. Life (as we know it) needs hydrogen, carbon, nitrogen and oxygen. There are traces of these up there but not enough to be turned into you or me or even **LITTLE BROTHERS**.

I'm not going to stick my neck out and say that we will or won't find tiny single-celled life but that's not what I'm looking for.

I told Kareem I was going to hunt for intelligent life and he asked me what I meant by intelligent.

I mean, duh. Like me. Like him.

$2H_2 + O_2 = 2H_2O$

Obviously.

Only, he took out his phone and showed me a video of a dolphin.

I said OK, yes but . . .

Then he showed me a video of a dog.

And then a video of an octopus.
And a crow.

I got the point.

So . . . maybe I'm not so
smart after all. I never thought about
what 'intelligent' **REALLY** means. It's
smart to build a spaceship but is it smart
to let people go hungry? Or cause climate
change?

Maybe, just maybe, the kind of aliens
I want to meet aren't going to be the type who
build spaceships or even phones.

Oh no. Imagine. A world without phones!
Talk about **ALIEN!**

OK, I can see now that not all intelligent
life will be space explorers, and that it would
be quite nice to find extra-terrestrial dolphins.
Consider my mind open to the possibilities.

Can I find life on any of the other planets in

our solar system? Are there Martians on Mars? Jovians on Jupiter? Or . . . nope . . . I don't even want to think about what's on Uranus.

All of those things are unlikely so what is it about this little rock we call Earth that makes it completely **BURST** with oodles of brilliant and exciting life forms?

The word I hear again and again when I ask anybody **'WHY EARTH'** is **'GOLDILOCKS'**. They all mean that some planets are too cold and some planets are too hot but Earth is **JUST RIGHT**.

Aww. How lovely.

And what a load of nonsense.

For a start, Goldilocks could have just stopped moaning about the food she was stealing and thanked her lucky stars there was food around. If my dinner is too hot, then I just wait a bit or blow on it. If it's too cold, then Dad says I shouldn't have been chatting so much and I can pop it in the microwave for a minute.

So don't get me started on Goldilocks.

The other thing about the 'just right' theory is that life is really good at staying alive. Explorers have discovered life in freezing seas and living in boiling water in deep parts of the ocean. They've even taken one type of life into space to see how it survives **WITHOUT AIR**. It's called a **TARDIGRADE**.

The tardigrade is a tiny creature — less than

a millimetre long — and looks like an armadillo. It can't build a spaceship but it is very tough. They aren't the only tough species around. There are more and they've all been grouped together and called **EXTREMOPHILES.**

This is totally the superhero movie I want to see next.

Life would need to be an extremophile in order to survive on any of the other planets in our solar system. I've written another list! I call this:

The House Hunter's Guide to Bad Neighbourhoods.

✦ MERCURY

Mercury is the planet closest to the Sun. It has a funny orbit which means one year is about **eighty-eight Earth days** whilst a solar day on Mercury lasts **176 Earth days**. Yes, you read that right. A day on Mercury is longer than a year.

What this means is that there is daylight on Mercury for **eighty-eight Earth days** and darkness for the remaining eighty-eight Earth days.

That's a long time to be in the Sun and that side of the planet gets really hot whilst the other (night-time) side gets really cold. Oh, and there's very little atmosphere. For life to exist in those conditions it would have to be very different to life on Earth.

Hey Goldilocks! Try complaining about your porridge on Mercury.

☆ VENUS

Venus isn't much kinder to life though. It's the second planet closest to the Sun but the hottest because it is entirely covered by clouds which keep all the heat in. Plus, there is a super dense atmosphere, which means the pressure at ground level is enough to crush even the toughest metals. Unless Flat Stanley has a second home on Venus then the only possible place for life to exist would be in the clouds. Maybe tiny organisms have evolved in there, but nobody really knows at the moment.

☆ MARS

Mars looked good for a while. Early photographs showed dark areas which people thought might be grasslands. Then we got better photos and then we sent probes there and realised it was a very cold, dry place. There may be water ice deep down, but nobody knows at the moment. What is interesting though is that there may have been rivers and lakes on the surface a couple of billion years ago. It's unlikely that there was enough time for complex life to evolve but imagine Mars looking like an early Earth! If only it could have kept its atmosphere, then maybe we'd already be talking to Martians.

✦ JUPITER

As you go further out it seems really unlikely that life could exist. Space is very cold and you're not going to evolve as a life form unless you're wearing the big jumper your gran knitted for you. Jupiter is an enormous planet held together by storms. There's no solid surface and there are regular storms reaching hundreds of kilometres per hour.

But the moons of Jupiter . . . well that's a whole other story.

Europa is one of Jupiter's **BIG FOUR**, also called the Galilean moons. Some of these are bigger than Mercury. Europa even has an ocean under its surface and because there is also heat (generated by Jupiter's gravity pulling at the moon) the ocean stays liquid. Which also means that there's a chance life might be able to live there.

Just maybe not dolphins.

It makes me wonder whether there really is such a thing as a 'Goldilocks zone'. I mean, I can see why some parts of a solar system will be more comfortable for our kind of life, but the universe is such a large place, and there are so many stars and planets out there, that life could evolve in all kinds of surprising ways.

Like, who could have predicted my little brother?

✬ SATURN

Saturn's surface is also a bit squidgy with terrifically fast storms. The clouds are **FREEZING COLD** but it does get warmer the further down you travel. Unfortunately, the pressures would be crushing. But just like Jupiter, Saturn has some interesting moons.

Enceladus is one of them. It could support life because (like Europa) it might have water —

and where there is water, there **MIGHT** be life because water is, like, super important to all life. Especially when there is heat.

URANUS

This is another of the wibbly-wobbly planets with no rocky surface. It's made mostly of ice – but not the nice kind of ice you take out of a freezer on a hot summer day. I've learned enough to never say **NEVER** but this wouldn't be the first place I'd go poking around for signs of life.

NEPTUNE

Like Uranus but with the dial turned up to eleven, Neptune is cold and inhosp . . . inhos . . . I can't spell 'inhospitable' so I'll just say it's **UNFRIENDLY**. The atmosphere is a very strange place and it's possible (**POSSIBLE**) that it rains diamonds. I say possible because nobody has definite proof. This sounds interesting and would look very pretty but I'm looking for **LIFE**.

Both Neptune and Uranus have no volcanic activity or way to generate heat. Life really does seem to like heat. Which brings me onto . . .

☆ PLUTO

Even Pluto, the dwarf planet, has some kind of heat which keeps things moving under its surface so is there life under the ice? It's such a faraway place and the Sun's heat barely reaches it, but heat isn't only produced by the Sun. It can be generated by other forces — such as pulling and twisting an object. I can test this theory by squeezing a rubber squash ball. The more I squeeze, the hotter it gets. Maybe something is going on deep inside Pluto to create heat or maybe the way Pluto's moon (Charon) orbits it creates some heat. We do know there is some heat. There are patterns on the surface which happen because of heat.

All this is intriguing my scientific brain but it's not really doing much for the intergalactic space explorer in me.

I need more ways to search for the perfect planet.

Chapter 11

MAGICAL SPACE UNICORNS

Listening for alien signals in the radio waves travelling across the universe is pretty awesome but seeing evidence of extra-terrestrial life with my own eyes would be even better.

The problem is that planets aren't all lit up. Even Earth isn't and it has big cities full of street and building lights. Our telescopes can see very distant stars because 1. stars are massive compared to planets, and 2. stars are super bright.

I have already learned that we can detect planets by listening to pulsars but yesterday I read that we could see planets by watching stars. I didn't understand how until I went to the cinema yesterday. I'm a **DO NOT TALK, EAT OR MOVE** film viewer, but my little brother was eating (though I was a little surprised that he

Me!

offered me some of his Galaxy bar), Dad was whispering to ask Mum what was happening, and then **SOMEONE** stood up and walked out.

I almost shouted **EUREKA** but then I remembered my **NO TALKING** rule.

The person's head blocked my view as they passed in front of the screen. I couldn't see what the person looked like, but I knew they were there because I could see their silhouette.

THAT is what I'd been reading about.

If I point a telescope at a star and just watch ... and watch ... and watch, eventually it might get a bit dimmer. If that happens then I know something has passed in front of it. By measuring how long it takes for the same thing to happen again (dimming by the same amount), I can figure out how big the object is and how far away from the star it must be.

Planet hunting in the dark.

A really good telescope to use to do this is called **KEPLER**. Or rather, it **WAS** called Kepler. The telescope ran out of fuel in 2018 but not before it found a whopping **2,662** planets. Those planets are called **EXOPLANETS** because 'exo' means 'from outside'. In this case, the outside is beyond our solar system.

It's all very amazing.

Once we know how far from the star a planet is, we can also tell if it's within that Goldilocks zone. I might no longer think this is the ONLY place where life could exist but it does seem the place where life is **MORE** likely to. So OK, Goldilocks, you can stay for now.

But wouldn't it be great if we could see whether that planet had an atmosphere capable of supporting life?

Luckily my dear friend the

ELECTROMAGNETIC SPECTRUM has

the answer to that.

The visible part of the spectrum is useful for helping us to avoid bumping into things. But, as I discovered when I learned about the expanding universe, the colour of light is useful too.

Today the sky is blue. Last night, just as the Sun was setting, it was red. Mum tells me that the Sun rises in the morning, but I've always been very busy at that time of the day. Very busy sleeping.

The reason the sky is blue (or red, or has any colour at all) is because the atmosphere scatters light in different ways. The molecules of oxygen and nitrogen in the air scatter the light with a shorter wavelength more than they scatter light with a longer wavelength. Light with a short wavelength is at the blue end of the spectrum whilst light with a longer wavelength is at the red end (as I learned with the red and blue shift effect of moving stars). The blue light gets smeared all over the place like chocolate on a baby's face. The more air light passes through the more it gets scattered. That's why it is even lighter blue at the horizon than it is directly overhead. The rest of the light (more towards the red end of the spectrum) is why the Sun appears yellowy-orange because that kind of light doesn't spread out as much. When the blue light gets scattered even more (like when the Sun is lower in the sky and there's more air to pass through) then the Sun and the sky becomes more red.

If the molecules in the air were something other than oxygen and nitrogen, then different wavelengths of light would show up.

A powerful telescope like Kepler can use the light from a distant star to see what colours are filtered out through its atmosphere. Just like when we split white light into a rainbow, so we can use those colours to measure the composition of the atmosphere. Every substance absorbs different wavelengths of light in different ways. It's like the rainbow fingerprint of a magical space unicorn.

The thing is, I really want to know what the chances are of finding life out there which is capable of talking to me, and perhaps cooking my tea.

Luckily, I found something which might help me figure that out.

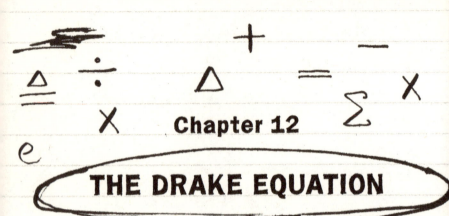

Chapter 12

THE DRAKE EQUATION

Before I make the journey all the way from the living room to the fridge, I do a very clever calculation to determine whether it's going to be worth the effort.

Last time Mum went to the shop.

Last time Dad went to the shop.

Last time Kareem 'accidentally' called in at teatime.

My hunger level since I woke up.

Each of these factors helps me figure out whether there will be anything worth eating. In Matilda's Made-Up Maths the equation might look like this:

$$F = (M - D) - K - H$$

I'd better explain. My maths can be complicated to the uninitiated.

F stands for **FOOD**. With me so far? I can break it down even further. By **FOOD** I mean quality snacks: cheesecake, jelly, chocolate bars (though I'd prefer if these **WEREN'T** kept in the fridge thank-you-very-much), cheese, cold pizza, and so on. I think you're on my wavelength* here.

---

* Check the Matildamunchtastic Spectrum chart on the next page to show the full range of acceptable snacks.

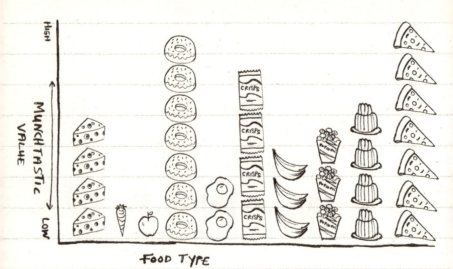

MUNCHTASTIC VALUE

HIGH

LOW

FOOD TYPE

M stands for **MUM** and **D** stands for **DAD**. The reason I've put a minus sign between them is that Mum buys **GOOD SNACKS** but Dad buys 'healthy' food and so those two parts can sometimes cancel each other out. Especially when we bring in the next bit . . . **KAREEM**.

Yep, **K** stands for Kareem. The value of **F** definitely goes down when Kareem calls in.

And then of course there's **H**, for **HUNGER**. My hunger. This number is derived (a fancy word for worked out) by looking at how long I've been out of bed and . . . well, that's probably all it is. If I've just woken up then there has only been one fridge raid. The longer I'm awake the more fridge raids I'll have been on.

So that's my equation. And the reason I'm writing it down is because it helps me to understand this equation:

$$N = R^* \times f_p \times n_e \times f_i \times f_i \times f_c \times L$$

This one has nothing to do with snacks. It was written down by a man called Frank Drake. We call it the Drake equation. He did it as a way to work out the chances of there being alien civilisations.

I still don't **REALLY** understand it. At least, I don't understand how to get the numbers for every bit. Honestly though, I don't think anyone else does either because lots of it sounds like guessing and I would get told to go back and do it again if I handed that in to my teacher.

This is what I do understand though.

N is the number of civilisations we might be able to talk to. That's the number I want to know. I'm easily pleased though because if **N = 1** or more then I'm happy and all set to pack a bag and hitch a ride on the USS Enterprise.

R* represents how many stars per year form in our galaxy. This is all about finding stars which might allow for the evolution of life.

f_p is how many of those stars have planets. Planets, as I've already deduced, are **VERY IMPORTANT.** I know I wouldn't have a home without one.

n_e is the number of planets in a solar system which are safe to live on. But here's a problem —

if life can exist in the most horrendously awful conditions (like a house with no cake) then how do we work **THAT** out?

!!!GUESS ALERT!!!

f_l is the number of THOSE planets where life has actually appeared . . .

f_i is the number of **THOSE** planets where **INTELLIGENT** life (whatever **THAT** means) has evolved. I think Kareem is right — we are so human-centric. We think we are the most intelligent species ever.

f_c is the number of civilisations which can hold up a sign saying **WE ARE HERE**. So I think this makes the previous number a bit easier

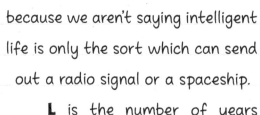

because we aren't saying intelligent life is only the sort which can send out a radio signal or a spaceship.

L is the number of years those civilisations have been sending out signals.

I think the entire point of this is to say there are a LOT of hoops to jump through. I mean, look at this planet. As everyone on one of the planets in the NGC 4845 galaxy will know from observing our planet as it was **65 million years ago**, LIFE IS HARD. One minute you're auditioning for a role in Jurassic Park and the next . . . WHAM! You're gone. Loads of species have become extinct during the history of life on Planet Earth. We've managed to hang on but there's been a lot of luck in that. Here's my PHEW list:

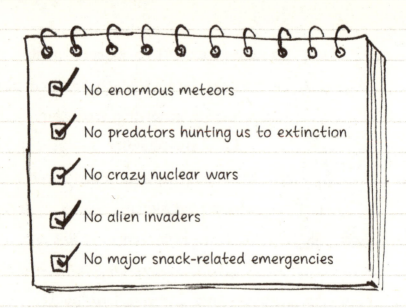

- ☑ No enormous meteors
- ☑ No predators hunting us to extinction
- ☑ No crazy nuclear wars
- ☑ No alien invaders
- ☑ No major snack-related emergencies

WELL DONE HUMANS!

We're not in the clear yet though. We really need to sort this planet out. Climate change means it's getting more difficult for life to exist comfortably on Earth. It might even become impossible unless we learn to stop polluting it and taking more than we need. But the good news is that you all have **ME!** And every other child. Because we are the future and we can make a difference. Oi! Dad! Let's ride our bikes instead of driving to the shops. Let's eat less meat and fish (and more cake).

Even though a lot of the numbers in that equation feel like wild guesses, the thing that's going in my favour is that there are a **LOT** of stars. In our galaxy there are at least **100 BILLION** of them. And there are at least **100 BILLION** galaxies in the observable universe. That's a lot of stars. Even if only **1%** of those stars have planets, then we're still talking **BIG NUMBERS**.

I know there's no absolute guarantee of there being another space-going civilisation out there but at least the numbers are on my side.

Or rather, some of the numbers are.

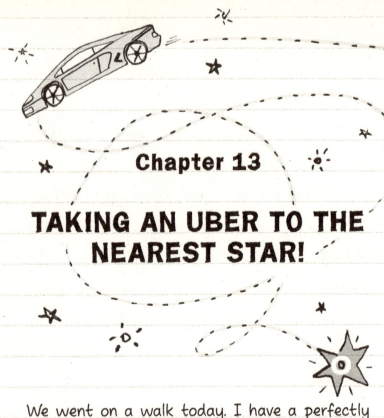

Chapter 13

TAKING AN UBER TO THE NEAREST STAR!

We went on a walk today. I have a perfectly good bike but for some reason, I had to use my legs. I'm not a walker. I once suggested ordering a pizza delivery when I was sitting in the school dinner hall because it was too far to walk to the serving hatch.

The walk today was my own fault. I made the mistake of talking to Kareem about how far it was to the edge of the solar system. He was excited and wanted us to test the maths. He's all about the maths.

METRE RULER

The problem is it involved walking and I really wasn't in the mood to walk to the edge of the solar system.

Kareem suggested we shrink the solar system down to a scale I could manage. We imagined Earth to be the size of a marble and the Moon was a ball of blu-tac about a quarter of the size. At that scale the Sun would have a diameter which equals the height of my little brother — about **a metre**. He came along with us too and I have to admit, he was kind of good fun to have around and didn't once ask to be picked up.

The closest planet to the Sun is Mercury. At our scale that meant walking **39 metres**. That wasn't so difficult. I felt like this was going to be the easiest walk ever. After all, the planets were tiny.

The next closest planet is Venus (and that's the hottest, remember). We had to walk even less this time. Just another **33 metres**, making our walk the grand old distance of **72 metres**. Happy times!

Next comes Earth. That meant walking

another **28 metres** (total leg stretching = **100 metres**). The distance to the Moon at this scale is less than a metre and yet (as I discovered when I tried to build a Saturn V) that distance is enough to fit all the other planets inside.

After Earth is Mars. That meant walking a bit more — but still only **52 metres** (we were at **152 metres** now).

Ok, so this was a bit further. Jupiter is the fifth planet in the solar system and that meant walking for **368 metres**. We were now

520 metres from the Sun.

Saturn was another **433-metre** walk, bringing us **953 metres** from the Sun. This was turning into a proper walk.

To get to Uranus I had to walk the same **ENTIRE** distance again. Another **947** metres which meant I'd walked **1.9 km** in total. On a real-world scale that's **2.8 BILLION km** and I felt Every. Single. **KILOMETRE.**

We're not finished yet.

Neptune is the last planet in the solar system. We walked.

And walked.

And walked.

It took us another **1.1 km** to reach Neptune. That's **3 km** from the Sun and I said there had better be a bus home.

At least we'd reached the edge of the . . .

hold on a minute. We didn't reach the edge of anything. Neptune is **4.5 BILLION km** from the Sun but there's still a long way to go.

After Neptune there is Pluto, a dwarf planet. We would need to walk another **kilometre** to reach it. That puts it at **FORTY** times the distance Earth is from the Sun. The distance between Earth and the Sun (a Sunday stroll now I've walked **4.5 billion km**) is **150 million miles** and it's often called an **AU**. We keep finding easy ways to keep the numbers down — metres rather than millimetres, kilometres rather than metres, AU rather than kilometres, light years rather than AU or kilometres.

Kareem asked me about Pluto and I love it when I can talk about something I just found out so I explained that Pluto has a very weird orbit which sits at a slant to all the other planets. It's part of the Kuiper belt — which is

kind of like the asteroid belt between Mars and Jupiter. These are objects that couldn't attract enough mass to become planets but which are still amazing. I think I'll find out a bit more about Pluto when I think about how we might travel these colossal distances.

But the real edge of the solar system is called the heliopause (helios means 'sun' in Greek). In **2012** Voyager 1, a spacecraft launched in **1977**, detected the edge.

This was **18 BILLION km** from the Sun. That's **FOUR** times further than I'd already walked. And there **MIGHT** be something called the Oort cloud beyond that. The Oort cloud (I just want to keep saying that) is a sphere of icy dust and rocks around the solar system. It could be where comets start their journey inward to orbit the Sun. The inner edge of the Oort cloud could be **2,000 AU** (remember, Pluto is **40 AU**) but the edge of the Oort could be as far away as **100,000 AU**.

MY FEET OORT. MY BRAIN OORTS.

Let's get Oort of here.

Kareem groaned at my joke but my little brother and I laughed.

So yeah, Kareem, my brother and I went on a walk today and we all learned that space is really big. Even our local bit of space.

To meet an extraterrestrial civilisation will involve some serious walking.

When I got back, I wanted to scribble down some notes to understand the distances in terms of the time it might take. The distance a planet is from Earth varies a **LOT** so I'm going to go for the average distance here. And I'm using a straight line.

One AU is the distance between the Sun and Earth. That means **1 AU** equals **149,598,000 km**. To keep things simple I'm saying the distance

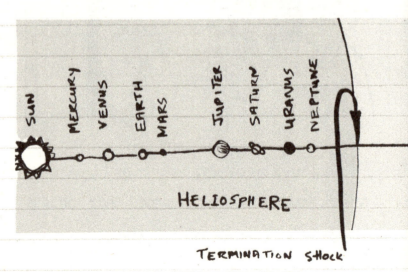

TERMINATION SHOCK

between each planet is current planet distance from Sun minus previous planet distance from Sun. I've already had my head stretched over the issue of average distances so I don't want to start going through that again because all I'm trying to show here is that the solar system is BIG and travelling about takes a long time.

Here are the distances between the Sun and each of the planets (and the edge of the solar system) in AU:

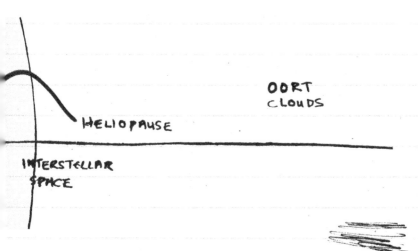

OORT
CLOUDS

HELIOPAUSE

INTERSTELLAR
SPACE

Mercury = 0.39

Venus = 0.72

Earth = 1

Mars = 1.52

Jupiter = 5.2

Saturn = 10

Uranus = 19.2

Neptune = 30.06

Heliosphere = 119

Still with me? Let's get motoring!

The speed limit on UK motorways is **70 miles per hour** which is about **112 km per hour**. If our car could travel in space, then at that speed it would take us **79 years** to reach Mars.

Even my brother would be grown up by then.

To get to Jupiter from Mars it would take another **561 years**, and from there it would take **661 years** to reach Saturn.

The distances really became clear when I worked out that to travel from Neptune to the edge of the solar system would take **10,682 years.**

Of course, no spacecraft would travel so slowly. Voyager 1 travels at **61,000 km per hour** which sounds **SUPER** fast. It sounds even crazier when I found out that means it covers **3.6 AU** each year — just over three and a half times the distance between Earth and the Sun. Such a long way!

And yet . . . Voyager took **40 years** to leave the solar system.

So how far is it to Proxima Centauri, the closest star to Earth?

Oh, only about **40,000,000,000,000 km** away. Or to put it in smaller numbers: just over **4 light years** away. That would be a journey of about **80,000 years** if I travelled at the same speed as Voyager is travelling.

That's not exactly a 'just popping out to see Kareem' distance.

Chapter 14

THE MOON
IS ALL MINE

To be honest, when I do visit Kareem, I treat it like an epic voyage. There are two sweet shops and a chippy between us and I find I can only complete the journey if I call into at least one of them on the way. It's like when people climb Everest and they set up base stations along the route so they can top up with hot chocolate and catch up on new episodes of Ordinary Sausage on YouTube. Then, and only then, do they have the strength to walk a bit further.

To launch people into space and get them to the Moon isn't as simple as it sounds (trust me I've tried, but Mum stopped me before I could use the baby-sized catapult on my little brother*).

* Kareem vanished very quickly when that happened, as though he had nothing to do with helping me.

The Saturn V was **110 metres** high and most of that was filled with fuel. In fact, there was something like **3,500,000 litres** of fuel.

THREE AND A HALF MILLION . . . to send three people to the Moon. And most of it was used to get them off the planet.

The reason for this is because **GRAVITY SUCKS** (it does!). The pull of Earth's gravity is so strong that it takes a lot of energy to escape it.

This makes me wonder about two things:

1. What if we didn't need to escape Earth's gravity?
2. What if we could refuel in space?
3. What if I'd tried a bungee rope hung from a satellite instead of the catapult?

Ok, that's three things, but I can't help thinking that my plan to launch the **LITTLE BROTHER OF ANNOYANCE** (even though I'm starting to think he's maybe not all that annoying) into space might have worked. Although, if it had worked then I'd be even more annoyed because he'd be up there before me.

To get around the need to escape Earth's gravity, spaceships would have to be built in space or on the Moon.

The Moon's low gravity (just look at the way astronauts jumped up there — it has one sixth the gravity of Earth) means that a spaceship would need a lot less fuel to launch. I know this because the lunar landers all lifted off from the Moon to bring the Apollo astronauts home and they had pretty small fuel tanks.

When I talk about the Moon with my friends, some of them say "Matilda, it's just a dull grey rock like the school playground" but they are wrong — the Moon is a really exciting and diverse place. Perfect, in fact, both for building spaceships AND for making rocket fuel.

The first brilliant natural resource is . . . **SUNLIGHT**. On Earth we have sunlight for twelve hours a day. But on the Moon the Sun will shine for two weeks before it becomes night-time for two weeks.

All that solar energy can be used **FOR FREE**.

The Moon has other resources too.

We can use the lunar 'soil' (called **REGOLITH**) to build with and to get oxygen out of. Regolith can be made into a ceramic-like material.

There's also (probably) water ice deep in the craters at the poles — especially the south pole. The Sun doesn't reach those parts so it's likely to be frozen solid (we can build ice shelters and snowmen!).

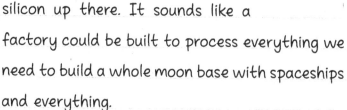

And the riches don't stop there.

There are metals like iron, aluminium, titanium and even silicon up there. It sounds like a factory could be built to process everything we need to build a whole moon base with spaceships and everything.

But that's kind of where my problem starts.

I love the idea of space travel so much. I think it's something that we need to do. But I don't want to get carried away because look at how much damage digging for stuff here on Earth is doing. We are running out of oil and some minerals and even if we weren't, the process of mining causes loads of problems —

like countries fighting to claim oil supplies and people living in terrible and unsafe conditions.

Do I really want the Moon to be turned into a massive mine?

Honestly, I don't know. I don't want to destroy the natural wonder of the Moon, but I can see how important it is in that next step to making humans an interplanetary species.

If we can learn to extract resources on the Moon (and I very much doubt it's as easy as sending Snow White and the Seven Dwarves up there to dig dig dig dig dig dig dig the whole day through) then we can learn to extract resources elsewhere in space.

Like from an asteroid.

An asteroid is a lump of rock that didn't become big enough to become a planet or a moon. That doesn't mean they are like bits of gravel or pebbles though. There is an asteroid in this solar system called Vesta which is **525 km** across (no, Kareem . . . I don't want to walk across it). And there is a dwarf planet (just like Pluto) in the asteroid belt called Ceres.

Asteroids can usually be found between Mars and Jupiter (in the asteroid belt) or beyond Neptune (in the Kuiper belt) but some have orbits which bring them close to Earth . . . and orbits change as one planet or another attracts them enough to nudge them onto a different path.

There are also objects called comets.

Whereas asteroids can be rock and metal, comets can be rock and ice. Comets come from much further out — beyond the Kuiper belt — and have long, elliptical orbits. From time to time, we get to see one in the sky and they are amazingly beautiful with long, dusty tails.

Not this kind of centaur!

And get this: there are even objects called . . . **CENTAURS**! How cool is **THAT**? A centaur can be like an asteroid or comet but with a much weirder orbit.

That means we don't need to completely wreck the Moon to get the materials for long space flights and, if it's a **REALLY** long spaceflight, then we can use asteroids and comets as base stations along the way.

And what a way it is.

Chapter 15

SPEEDING THINGS UP A BIT

Remember when I said that to get to the nearest star (after the sun) would take me **80,000 years**? Well before I agree to set out upon such an epic journey, I'm going to need some guarantees. Here are my demands.

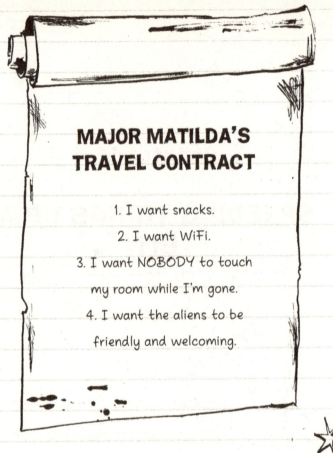

MAJOR MATILDA'S TRAVEL CONTRACT

1. I want snacks.
2. I want WiFi.
3. I want NOBODY to touch my room while I'm gone.
4. I want the aliens to be friendly and welcoming.

And of course, I need to know that there will be actual aliens on any planet I visit. If the **SETI** project hears a radio broadcast, then I'm sure **NASA** will phone me and arrange to pick me up on the next interstellar flight, but I can't rely on just one project.

I need **OPTIONS**, people, **OPTIONS**.

Sputnik 1 (**BEEP BEEP BEEP BEEP**) didn't search for life in space but it was the beginning of something special. Thanks to that we now have satellites which keep an eye on the climate, make the mapping apps work on our phones, and even explore the other planets (and asteroids) in our solar system.

Sending a probe to other planets works really well. There's a lot of risk sending people into space, but robots can learn a lot for us. Or we could send my little brother — although to be honest, the more I moan about him the more I think maybe I'm being a bit unfair. I would miss him. A bit. Maybe.

ANYWAY. The point is that there have been **LOADS** of robot explorers on Mars. These are little buggy-type robots known as rovers with names like Curiosity, Perseverance, Opportunity, and Matilda*. They've told us a lot about the planet's climate and what makes Mars tick.

Perseverance has been searching for signs of life by testing the soil but hasn't found any so far. The rovers are sent instructions by people on Earth and it's like a really slow video game because of **THE SPEED OF LIGHT** — which, it turns out, is frustratingly slow.

I know that it takes a while for light to travel through space. That's why over on **NGC 4845** my imaginary alien observers are only **JUST** seeing the dinosaurs go extinct. The thing is, I never really thought about how important this is — even for nearby stuff like rovers on Mars.

The speed of light is **299,792.458 km per second**. Which sounds **INSTANT** because it takes

---

* Not really but maybe I need to figure out how to build one.

This is Perserverance!

me about 10 minutes to run the 100 metres in school. Hey, so what? I like to stop and chat.

Light from the Sun takes roughly eight and a half minutes to cross the **150 million kilometres** between there and our planet (**1 AU**). That means if someone decided to switch off the Sun then we wouldn't know about it for eight and a half minutes.

But because everything on the **ELECTROMAGNETIC SPECTRUM** travels at the speed of light that also means if I decided to talk to someone who was stood upon the Sun then my urgent message of **"WEAR SUN CREAM"** wouldn't reach them for **eight and a half minutes**. I'm going to spend the rest of the day worrying about them now.

When we talk to the rovers on Mars then it takes a while for our radio signal (travelling at the speed of light) to be received.

Planets move around the Sun. And all that moving makes working out how far away they are quite tricky.

There's a **REALLY** weird thing which happens when we talk about average distances in space. The distance between a planet and the Sun varies, but not a lot because the Sun remains roughly in the same position. That means Earth will **ALWAYS** be about **150,000,000 km** from the Sun. But the distances between Earth and Mars (for example) vary way way more.

Sometimes Earth and Mars will be on opposite sides of the sun and sometimes they will be on the same side. When we look at the average, we have a lot more variation.

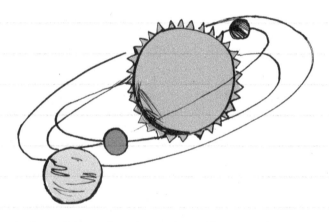

When Mars (or any planet) is on the same side of the Sun as Earth then it's going to be closer than if we are on opposite sides. That means the time it will take for a signal to reach a rover on Mars will change so I want to think what the average time might be (knowing that sometimes it will be more and sometimes less).

Another weird example of this is that on average Mercury is the planet which is closest to **EVERY OTHER PLANET**. That's because it spends more time on the same side of the Sun as the other planets.

Let's get back to our rover and something simple — like the speed of light.

The average distance between Earth and Mars is **225 million km**. That's the same distance as the distance between the Sun and Mars.

Here's how I work out the time it would take for a signal to reach the rover.

For this sum I'm going to round the speed of light up from **299,792.458 km per second** to **300,000 km per second**. The result (according to my maths) looks like this:

225,000,000 km divided by **300,000 km/s** = **750 seconds**.

750 seconds is the same as **12.5 minutes**.

That's how long it would take to shout at the rover

WATCH OUT FOR THAT ALIEN.

Then I'd need to wait the same amount of time for the reply.

Light is a bit of a slowcoach but it's the only coach we've got — at the moment.

When Voyager took **forty years** to leave the solar system, it was travelling at about **61,000 km per hour** which is WAY slower than the speed of light (but still faster than me doing the **100 metres**).

That **40,000,000,000,000 km** journey to Proxima Centauri might take a while. And even when I get there, sending a message back to Earth will take **four years**.

I can't do anything about the message time but there has to be a way to get there faster.

Weirdly, there is. It's being developed as a way to send another robot probe and it involves using light and a massive sail.

When I read about this, I thought **GREAT**. One phone call later and Jerome, Simone, and Kareem met me on the field near our houses. I brought along a massive bed sheet, two sticks, a skateboard, and a torch. Jerome is the lightest of us so he stood on the skateboard and we made a sail using the sheet and the sticks.

I shone the torch whilst Kareem listed a million reasons why this wouldn't work. He's helpful like that.

But he wasn't wrong. Nothing happened. Jerome wobbled a bit but I don't think that was because of the torch doing anything except getting in his eyes.

It turns out that light **CAN** move objects but only really really . . . **LIGHT** ones. Whilst we were trying the torch, Kareem did some proper research and discovered how it is supposed to work.

He told me about an Earth-sized planet orbiting Proxima Centauri. It's called Proxima Centauri b which is a very dull name. The planet

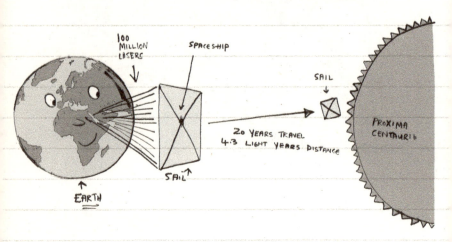

is in the 'Goldilocks zone' though so that's why it's been chosen. Kareem said the mission is called Breakthrough Starshot and it involves a thousand fist-sized and very light spaceships being launched into space. There they would unfurl huge (and also very light) sails. Very powerful laser beams (about a billion of them) would boost the spaceships to **20%** of the speed of light. That's a **LOT** faster than Voyager is travelling and it would mean the swarm of ships would take **twenty years** to reach the planet. They'd be going so fast, however, that they would whizz past but not before they took a load of photos and beamed them back to Earth.

This idea isn't likely to help me to reach other solar systems anytime soon. But it would be amazing to see photos of a new planet within my lifetime.

Jerome loves photography and said that new photos of old things could be amazing too. Simone seems to know everything Jerome knows and she said there was a spaceship in **2015** called New Horizons which took new photos of Pluto (up until then the best we had were taken from way back here on Earth).

New Horizons was travelling so fast and didn't slow down but still managed to take enough photos in such incredible detail that we know so much more about this weird little dwarf planet. The photos revealed a huge, icy-white, heart-shaped feature on the surface of Pluto. There are patterns on Pluto's 'heart' (called Sputnik Planitia) that match the pattern of a type of cloud on Earth which forms when hot air from the ground hits cold air in the sky. Because of this, scientists believe that there could be an ocean beneath the ice and that it's kept warm somehow. The rest of Pluto is covered in craters and Sputnik Planitia should be too, unless something is renewing that part of the surface.

If a superfast flyby can show us all that then Breakthrough Starshot will be very exciting.

But I'd still really like to visit another planet which might be home to a new civilisation.

Pluto's heart

Chapter 16

ROAD TRIP!

The answer to visiting other planets in distant solar systems might be to go on one brilliant, long, summer holiday. I've been on holidays which I never wanted to end. Not because I don't like school (I love school!) but because Mum doesn't worry about bedtimes or the number of ice creams I eat.

Imagine if we just kept travelling.

It's time to summon the family!

I call Great-Grandad, Grandma, Grandad, Mum, and Dad and sit them down at the kitchen table (I include the tortoise too, of course). Mum says she thought I wanted the entire family so after a bit of a grumble I let my little brother sit down too. He gave me a big smile.

We're going into space, I explain. And I want to know how you feel about it. We'd be gone forever and never see Earth again.

Great-Grandad wants to know who will water his goldfish.

Grandma and Grandad want to invite friends of theirs along. They like playing Fortnite and need some serious competitors.

Mum starts calculating how much lettuce to bring for the tortoise and Dad rushes upstairs to fetch spare socks.

I don't think they are taking this seriously.

Except, annoyingly, for my brother. He has been asking me **WHY** every two minutes for the last three years (or so it seems) but now he made sense.

He wanted to know why we were going into space. And then he wanted to know why we weren't coming back. And then he asked why we couldn't just nip to a planet and be back in time for tea (I did the whole light speed and almost unimaginable distance between stars talk for him).

The best thing about going on this road trip is that it would keep us all together. We get along great as a family so we'd be off to a good start. We would need to take other people though. The spaceship I'm thinking of is called a generational ship and that means not just great-grandparents, grandparents, parents and children but also grandchildren and great-grandchildren and great-great-grandchildren and great-great-great-grandchildren and **SO ON** until we finally reach our destination.

Imagine getting on a boat and knowing that you wouldn't reach dry land but that a thousand years later, your descendants would. That's what would happen with a generation ship. I'd be spending my entire life in space.

It sounds both amazing and a bit scary. I want to meet aliens, but the distances don't lie

SPACE IS BIG.

Even if me and my family (and a whole bunch of friends) agreed to do this, there are a lot of problems to figure out.

The Sun sends out solar radiation which can be harmful to everyone on Earth. The atmosphere helps protect us from a lot of it, but we use sun cream and sensible hats to help a bit more. If we lived on the Moon or on Mars, then we'd need to take even more care.

But the Sun also protects us from other forms of radiation. It wraps the entire solar system in a magnetic shield which helps deflect that radiation. Going into space between the planets in our solar system would be dangerous but leaving it would be riskier still.

We can solve this with proper shielding, but the problems don't end there.

Mum is right to think about how much lettuce to bring. We all need to eat (not just lettuce though, PLEASE). Scientists onboard the

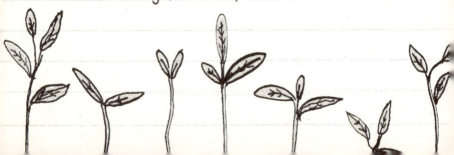

International Space Station have had success growing food in space, but it isn't easy and we will need to grow a lot. And to keep growing it.

Even Dad made sense when he went to grab spare socks. If we are going to create a society — even a small one — to last a thousand years, then we will all need a change of clothing.

And Great-Grandad's point about watering the goldfish? OK, that made no sense at all. But I love him anyway.

Water and (ahem) **BODILY WASTE** will need to be recycled and we'd need the skills to keep everyone healthy. That means looking after each other if we are sick but also helping babies be born and (sadly) being ready for when people die.

Humans are not designed to live in space. Mum says she sometimes wonders if I'm designed to live anywhere except a library or my bed.

And of course, just because my family gets along fine NOW doesn't mean future generations will. That's why we need a system of laws and enough police to make sure everyone follows them.

The good news is that one thing which would be useful to take with us is already packed: seeds.

When we get to a new planet, it would be very nice to start making it friendly to humans (as long as that doesn't mean upsetting anyone who lives there already). Planting trees and flowers and crops would be a start. Luckily a place in Norway called the Svalbard Global Seed Vault has begun saving seeds from all around the world, just in case they are needed.

I can see that to fit in everything we'd need to take, this spaceship would have to be bigger than the Apollo 11 command module I

once tried to build. That was about the size of a family car and three people had to fit in for a journey which lasted no more than **eight days**.

I can't see that working for a population of tens or even hundreds who live out their lives in it.

So maybe there's another solution to the long road trip:

FREEZING.

There's been an ice lolly in our freezer since before I was born. I once tried to pull it out, but it was stuck and even though I did my best King Arthur on it, it wouldn't budge. Mum says she doesn't remember who put it there and that there were now legends about it.

We could probably do something similar for travelling through space.

The science is called cryogenics and the idea is to put people into a kind of deep, frozen, sleep for as long as the journey takes. It sounds scary and the truth is that we don't have the skills to do it very well at the moment — but nature does.

There are animals which can freeze to the point where they seem dead but then thaw out when it gets warmer. And of course (OF COURSE) those tardigrades can withstand the process of freezing.

I'm beginning to think we should just teach tardigrades to talk and then send them out on a tiny spaceship of their own.

Amazing as cryogenics is though, spaceflight is going to take years. What I really need is a shortcut.

Chapter 17

DOWN THE RABBIT HOLE

One of the things I want to invent is a teleporter. That would be a machine which could reduce an object (or a body) into pure information and then send it as a signal to another machine anywhere else for it to be reassembled into matter.

Imagine being able to get to the fridge without having to walk down the stairs!

A teleporter wouldn't solve my interplanetary problems though. Information can still only travel at the speed of light — there's nothing faster. But maybe, just maybe, if there was some kind of tunnel through space then I could use that.

Luckily there is.

Sort of.

It's called a wormhole and much as I think that doesn't sound the nicest thing to crawl through, it could be an option.

To understand wormholes, I need to find out a bit more about Albert Einstein because it's his work which made people think they might exist.

Einstein was the man who said:

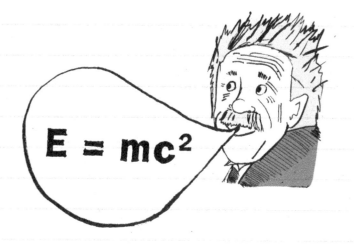

$$E = mc^2$$

And I nod along as though I know exactly what that means. Honestly though, I don't.

Kareem is working on a **TOP SECRET** project and even he says it's not easy to figure out. He says that it's a mistake to call space . . . **SPACE**.

Huh?

It goes like this: I know I move around in three dimensions. This is easily demonstrated when I get up out of bed, go down the stairs, turn left into the living room and then turn right into the kitchen. Ah, says Kareem, but you are forgetting the fact that whenever I move, I'm also moving through **TIME**.

So OK. It's not space, it's **SPACETIME**. If I go to the Moon, then I'm travelling through space**TIME**. I can't move **ONLY** through space because everything takes time.

The thing is, and this is what Einstein worked out, spacetime isn't flat. Wherever there is gravity, spacetime becomes warped. A little gravity barely makes a difference but something massive can make a lot of difference.

A black hole is the most powerful example of gravity we know of. **NOTHING**, not even a teenager trying to get out of doing the dishes, can escape its pull. Light is the fastest thing there is and not even **THAT** can escape its dark clutches <evil laugh>.

A black hole will warp spacetime so much that even time starts acting weird (I know the feeling). This led scientists to suggest that there also might be something called a white hole (I wonder if they come in other flavours too).

If a black hole draws things **IN** then a white

hole pushes them **OUT**. Nothing can escape a black hole, but nothing can enter a white one.

A wormhole might be created by connecting a black hole (in you go) to a white hole (out you pop). It's called an Einstein-Rosen bridge.

Another way to picture this is by taking a piece of paper (let's call that piece of paper **SPACETIME**) and folding it in two. Then stick a pencil through it. That hole is the wormhole and we've just folded the fabric of **SPACE AND TIME** to create a shortcut to anywhere in the **UNIVERSE** <evil laugh>.

Of course, even though it's one of the kinda-maybe-possibly-might-be-theoretically possible things, nobody has figured out how to make one otherwise I'd be writing this from a sandy beach on the planet Matilda IV.

That sounds bonkers, even by my standards. So at least I can fall back on **FASTER THAN**

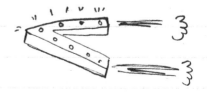

LIGHT travel . . . can't I?

I've seen it done a million times — in movies. One push of a button and

* z0000000000M

star systems whizz past the screen.

You. Can't. Travel. Faster. Than. Light. The. END.

At least, not through regular spacetime.

But why?

You can't push a beam of light any faster than the speed of light. If you are riding a bike and switch your torch on, then the beam of light is still moving at the same speed. It's not going light + bike because everything is measured relative to the object it's standing on.

Earth is orbiting the sun at roughly **107,000 km per hour**. We can even work that out because the orbit is more or less circular. I know that the circumference of a circle is equal to **2 x π x r**. I know **r** stands for radius which in this case is the radius of the Earth's orbit. That's the same as the distance to the sun (which is one **AU** or **150,000,000 km**). π is a value I know too — it's **3.142** (and an infinite number of digits after that).

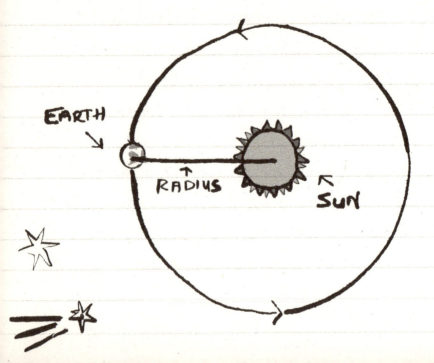

2 x 3.142 x 150,000,000 = 942,600,000.

I can divide that by **365** (the number of days in a year) and get the answer of **2,582,465.** That's how many kilometres Earth travels in a day. If I divide that number by **24** I get **107,602 km per hour**.

I enjoyed that!

Anyway, my point is that even though Earth is whizzing through space, the speed of light is still about **300,000 km per second**.

It's a constant.

But here's another thing, the most important thing actually. Light can move that fast because it has no mass. Light is made up from photons. What's a photon? A photon is a particle which has energy and movement but no mass or electrical charge. I, on the other hand, contain mass AND energy. Which is my standard excuse for why I move so slowly.

In almost all things, mass and energy are connected. The amount of energy I have is connected to my total mass and the speed of light. But not just the speed of light, the speed of light SQUARED (which means multiplied by itself).

To write that another way:

Energy = Mass x the speed of light **SQUARED**

Or

E = mc²

Energy is measured in **JOULES**, and mass is measured in **KILOGRAMS** and they are connected (just look at that big **EQUALS** sign for a clue).

When I move, I generate kinetic energy — which is the energy of movement. The problem is that the more kinetic energy I generate the more it affects my mass.

The closer I get to lightspeed the more kinetic energy I gain. This increases my mass.

But as my mass increases so does the energy I need to accelerate it. The effort gets harder and harder until it actually becomes impossible.

I should be talking about my spaceship here, not 'me'. I'm unlikely to Captain Marvel my way across the universe.

Remember the light sails in Breakthrough Starshot? The energy for moving all those tiny spaceships was given to them by firing the lasers at it. And it takes an enormous amount of energy to move something that small.

It seems as though the only way to visit planets in other solar systems will involve wormholes, generation ships, robot explorers, or something we haven't yet figured out.

Phew. That was WAY more sciencey than I

expected. I'm going to eat some ice cream and then tomorrow I think I'll draw a picture of an alien.

Chapter 18

NO, YOU LOOK LIKE AN ALIEN

I'm working on my magnificent first contact greeting. I can't decide whether to bow, high five, or shake hands with my new alien friends.

I guess a lot depends on the moment. If they are smiling, then maybe I'll go all chilled out with a high five but if they are frowning then I'll bow respectfully. I'm very good at understanding people's body language.

UPDATE: Kareem saw this journal on my bed and read that I said I was good at understanding body language. He made me write that I am not good at this and have more than once managed to annoy him by talking and talking and TALKING when he was sitting with his eyes closed trying to concentrate.

So OK, maybe I'll let the aliens make the first move.

The problem is what if they don't smile, or frown? What if they don't have mouths, or even faces as I understand them? What if they are, hmm, what's the word? ALIEN?

WHAT?

HA HA HA!

Kareem said it earlier when he asked me why I assumed the only intelligent life form was a human one. I keep thinking that in order to build civilisations, aliens (or extra-terrestrial non-human entities as it might be better to refer to them as) must look more or less like me.

But the extra-terrestrial non-human entities or — ENHEs — No, that's not going to work, is it? I'll call them aliens for now. The aliens might have evolved very differently depending upon the demands of their planet.

An octopus doesn't look like me (Kareem is reading over my shoulder and just said they look a little bit like me!). That's because they evolved to live in the sea (but with the ability to leave the water for short periods of time).

What would an alien look like?

It isn't just whether we live in the sea or in the air or on the land which changes the way

we look. Even the air we breathe will shape us.

When I was trying to build a Saturn V I learned that the air we breathe is made of three main parts: oxygen, nitrogen and carbon dioxide. Our blood needs oxygen but because of the air pressure here on Earth, we can't breathe pure oxygen. We've adapted to the mix around us.

It didn't start that way.

More than three billion years ago, the air was made mostly of carbon dioxide with methane and ammonia. This was because of all the volcanoes spewing out those gases. We can't breathe that stuff now but back then life forms could.

Over time, Earth chilled out a bit and the mix in the air became more like it is today — mostly nitrogen with a hefty helping of oxygen and far far less carbon dioxide. Yum!

So how did the oxygen get here? Well, some

Lots of methane and ammonia spurts out of here!

of those early life forms did what plants do today — they photosynthesised. Oxygen was the stuff they released into the atmosphere just as carbon dioxide is the stuff we release.

That wouldn't be enough to do the job of changing the air mix, but they had help. Carbon dioxide became trapped in the oceans and in the dead bodies of shellfish and plants. These became fossil fuels and one reason why more carbon dioxide is being released these days is because we are burning fossil fuels in our cars and homes and aeroplanes, which release it back into the atmosphere.

If the atmosphere had remained thick with smoke and carbon dioxide, then evolution would have taken a different path. Or maybe life just wouldn't have survived for very long.

I think there's no real way to tell what alien life might look like. If the gravity of their planet is higher than ours then any bones and muscles which evolve would need to be stronger than ours. Or maybe the life forms wouldn't walk on two legs but be more like lizards.

When I was researching what the planets in our solar system looked like, I discovered that on Neptune it is possible for the rain to be made of diamonds. As amazing as this sounds, and as much as I want to launch a mission there **IMMEDIATELY** (I'll pay for the spaceship when I get back), I'm slightly more interested in how to protect myself against razor sharp diamond rain. If life evolved on Neptune, then that's another thing it would need to figure out.

I asked Dad what he thought aliens might look like and he said "little green men". I mean, that's so obvious. Every dumb TV show makes them look that way. I said that, but Dad said I should think about it a bit more — and especially how photosynthesis was important (and IS important) to making life possible.

Photosynthesis is the way chlorophyll in a plant converts carbon dioxide and water into sugars. The energy it needs to do this comes from the light. And **GUESS WHAT**? Chlorophyll absorbs red or blue light best. It reflects green light (I knew reading about the **ELECTROMAGNETIC SPECTRUM** would come in handy). That's why leaves are green.

If an alien life form got its energy this way then maybe it would have green skin.

Don't tell Dad but he seems to have made a good point.

The other thing I thought about when trying to decide what aliens would look like is that I can't even guess what life looks like on Earth.

Seriously.

Who would have drawn an octopus? Or a pangolin? Or a proboscis monkey?

If I've learned anything then it's that life

is always ALWAYS surprising. If it can begin next to super-hot volcanic vents beneath the ocean, thrive in extreme cold, or even adapt to survive in the airless vacuum of space, then I think it would be very bizarre for it to only exist on Earth.

All life forms that we have found on Earth are made of

hydrogen, carbon, nitrogen and oxygen. The great news is that all of these elements can be found all over the universe so it's likely there is life (of some sort) out there too. It's like if we find evidence of flour, eggs, sugar and water on other planets then there's a good chance that there are cakes.

I know the distances involved mean that making contact with other life forms is more difficult, but at least the chances of there being other life forms is high.

I was going to end my thoughts on me finding alien life right there but a word just leaped out at me and it's one I've written before:

CONTACT.

I've discovered how SETI is listening for alien communication but contact means asking how I will actually talk to an alien.

Chapter 19

SAY WHAT?

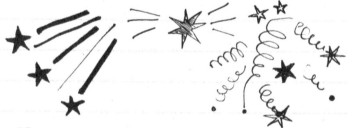

"Do you want chicken on your sandwich?"

"I've never been to Turkey."

"It won't be warm."

"The hand dryers in Jodrell Bank used to be marvellous."

This is a typical conversation between my Dad and my Grandad. It makes no sense. I'm not even going to explain who said which part because it still wouldn't make sense. Yet they both manage to talk about holidays and make sandwiches together without actually listening to one another.

My brother can be annoying (as I've mentioned here many times) but then every now and again he will run up and give me a hug and it's like he can read my mind and know that I needed a hug at that exact moment.

Language is weird. Sometimes we communicate with words and sometimes we don't.

Yesterday I was thinking about how I'd talk to an alien. At first, I thought that maybe

it would be like learning another language. Mum speaks six languages and she says it's not just the words that change but also the way of thinking. Take tenses. I can say "I opened the fridge" or "I'm opening the fridge" or "I will open the fridge". There's also a very tense expression in our house which is "I'll be in trouble for opening the fridge".

Past, present, future.

Not all languages on Earth do this. Some have more tenses and some have none.

But language on Earth has evolved through people interacting in certain ways and because of certain needs*.

On another planet those ways and needs would be completely different. Maybe the entire

* I wonder whether the very first word was "RUN".

method of communicating would be baffling to me. Maybe they talk in numbers or equations. Maybe there are no words — lots of animal species manage to communicate without anywhere near as complex a language as the one I use.

There are over **7,000 languages** in the world. Some are spoken and written, some are only spoken, some only written, and some are signed. Just as with the amazing diversity of appearances of life on Earth, language seems pretty varied too.

What chance do I have of talking with an alien?

I was trying to get my little brother out of my room when I realised something about myself that I don't like. I've spent AGES learning all about the universe, how it was made, how big it is, how it works, and what the chances of life on other planets might be but I've been unfair to my little . . . to Harry.

I need to stop calling him my little brother or HE WHO SHALL NOT BE NAMED.

He is called Harry and I realise that when he's hanging around, he's only trying to learn how to communicate with me.

If I'm ever going to talk with aliens, then I need to start by learning how to be a bit more patient with him. I need to learn how to listen. His use of language is still different to my own and I don't always remember that.

We can start by finding things in common.

When the two Voyager spacecraft were launched* in **1977**, they carried with them a golden disc. On each disc were examples of music, stories, and language. Engraved on the disc were pictures of what people look like and some things which the scientists hoped would be common to anyone who might find the spacecraft.

---

* Voyager 1 was launched on September 5, 1977. Voyager 2 was launched on August 20th, 1977. Both had a mission to explore the outer planets and then go beyond into interstellar (between stars) space.

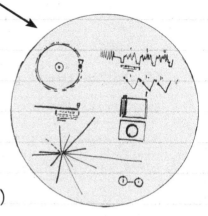

The golden disc.

The chance of anyone finding either Voyager craft is tiny — they are about the size of a small car (NASA seems to build a lot of things at this size) and, as I've already learned, space is BIG. But there is a chance and I think it's a wonderfully hopeful thing to have done.

One of the things on the disc was something which scientists thought ANYONE could recognise: a diagram of a hydrogen atom.

Hydrogen is the simplest and most common atom in the universe. The hope is that anyone understanding that can begin to piece together some of the other information on the disc — including instructions for how to play the sounds on the golden disc.

That's the thing about science — it's true no matter where you are in the universe. A star works the same way in our solar system as it would in any other solar system. It's the same with maths. There are different ways of working things out, but the answers are going to be the same.

If I start from these things, then I think I can build an understanding from there. It's all about being ready to learn how other people think. That goes as much for a life form which builds interstellar generation ships as it does for an octopus living in the ocean.

If Mum can understand what the tortoise needs, then I'm sure I can work out what an alien is trying to tell me — if it wants to tell me anything. Because that's another thing. I can't expect other life forms to be as keen to make contact as I am. I'd need to be respectful of

their ways and not just turn up with a suitcase saying "HI, I'M MATILDA AND I'VE COME TO LIVE WITH YOU AND SHOW YOU MY POKÉMON COLLECTION."

Though they'd be daft not to want to see it.

Mostly though I'm looking around this little planet of ours and wondering if we couldn't all benefit from learning to talk to one another in a better way.

And this makes me think a bit more about wanting to find aliens.

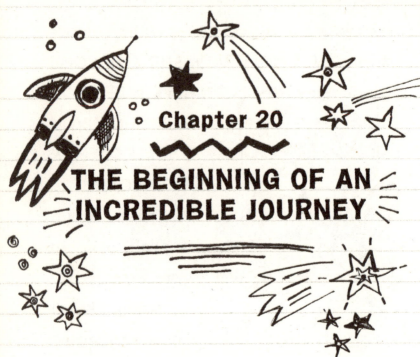

Chapter 20

THE BEGINNING OF AN INCREDIBLE JOURNEY

I used to think that my journey to the stars would begin when I put on my space helmet, tucked my teddy into my utility belt* and waved goodbye to my family. Or, if they were coming with me, when I put them into deep

---

* Astronauts don't really have a utility belt but I'm going to start a trend.

cryogenic sleep and started to help myself to the ice cream.

Then I thought that maybe it would begin when I learned enough to know what to expect.

But now I think I was wrong.

My journey didn't begin when I learned how big the universe was (**93 billion light years** across).

It didn't begin when I learned that the universe we talk about is only the observable universe — and that there might be more, FAR more than that.

It didn't begin when I learned about the number of stars in the Milky Way (at least **100 billion**)

OR the number of galaxies in the (observable) universe (at least **100 billion** of those).

It didn't begin when I realised that many of those stars would have planets and a good number of those would be capable of supporting life.

It didn't begin when I read all about how tough life is, and how it can adapt to survive in even the harshest conditions here on Earth.

It didn't begin when I understood how long it takes to leave our solar system, and then how long it would take even the fastest spacecraft to reach the nearest star (**four light years** away).

It didn't begin with learning about the challenges of finding alien life or of learning to talk to it.

It didn't begin when I learned that I might

need to pack my family onto a spaceship and actually **NEVER** reach the end of my journey.

It didn't even begin when I decided to keep a journal to record everything I've learned.

All of those things have been wonderful milestones in my journey, but I think it began in a different place.

Like, maybe, **13.8 billion years ago** when I was part of a soupy mix of quarks and gluons. Hey, maybe we knew each other! Maybe we shared a Planck!*

It may have taken a while but eventually, after a whole load of stars formed and exploded and scattered more complex atoms across the

---

* This is a very clever joke because Planck is the name given to the very smallest possible unit of measurement but it also sounds like 'plank' which is just a length of wood. I'm so funny!

universe, and after these found their way onto the third rock from our sun and evolved into organic life, I settled into the shape I am today and began to learn all I could learn about the universe.

And the amazing thing is: my journey is really still only getting started — even after **13.8 billion years**.

And even then, it will barely have begun.

It will continue long after the me I see in the mirror is old. Even after **5 billion years** have passed and the Sun has become a white dwarf*. And even after the stars in the Milky Way begin to go cold.

When I was learning how to build my own Saturn V I read about the first law of thermodynamics which was first written down by Rudolf Clausius. He said that energy is neither created nor destroyed, it just changes state. Everything is a form of energy so this law means that even though things might die, the energy they contain just becomes something else. In other words, everything that ever was and ever will be, exists now. It existed at the moment of the Big Bang and maybe even before. So when I die, my energy will be the spark for something else. Like, the energy which pushes oxygen through my blood will power

* The sun is going to cool and become a red giant which fills the space between where it is and where Mars is. Then it will shrink to become a white dwarf. This will happen in 5 billion years, so set your alarm clocks.

heat in the air or help bacteria grow in the soil. The energy which holds together molecules in my bones will move on to be part of something else.

When the universe is cold and no more stars can form, that energy will still be there — it will just be so spread out that it can't pull itself together again. Which is pretty much how Dad likes to describe me and my room when he's trying to wake me at 7am.

That's why I'm going to make the most of it.

I'm going to look at the universe around me. That means the sky above my head, the land beneath my feet, and the oceans which flow around it. I'm going to keep asking questions about the stars, like why are they different colours* and how many cheesy crisps can I fit into my mouth**.

There are LOADS of things I want to find

out. And I still want to build a spaceship —
or rather, I'd like to be part of a team which
builds one.

But I don't want to miss out on the
wonderful, alien (and by that, I mean 'different
to me') experiences available on Earth. Maybe my
next adventure is to the bottom of the ocean.
Or maybe it's to be found right here at home.

I expect that I will meet many wonderful
things along the way.

*   The colour of a star depends on what temperature
     it is and what it's made from. Remember the
     electromagnetic spectrum? Well, that can help us
     understand what it's made from. A really hot star
     will be mostly blue, whilst a cooler star will be red.
**   Twenty, according to my most recent experiment.

GLOSSARY*

⭐ **AGE OF THE UNIVERSE SINCE THE BIG BANG: 13.8 billion years**. I want to ramble on a bit more because that answer feels too easy so I'll just tell you that our tortoise is called Flat and nobody knows how old he is. Or even if he is a he.

⭐ **ASTEROID:** An asteroid is a lump of rock floating about in space. They aren't big enough to be called moons or planets.

⭐ **ATOM:** An atom is the smallest whole thing that everything else is made of. There are

* Posh word for my notes about the tricky stuff in my journal.

smaller things but they always join together
to form an atom.

AU: AU is not something you say to someone
— it's the distance between Earth and the
Sun and is a handy way to measure other
distances. That distance can also be written as
150,000,000 km.

BIG BANG: This is the name we give to the
start of our universe. It's the process of all
the matter starting to clump together to
form atoms (and from that — everything else).

CENTAURS: Centaurs are small icy objects
in space (usually found between Jupiter and
Neptune) which have weird orbits. They aren't
planets but they're also not asteroids.

★ **CIRCUMFERENCE:** The circumference is the distance around an object.

★ **DIAMETER:** The distance from one edge of an object to the other.

★ **DIAMETER OF THE OBSERVABLE UNIVERSE:** The furthest distance we can see in any direction is **46.5 billion light years**. Therefore, the diameter (if you fancy going for a walk one day) is **93 billion light years**.

★ **DOPPLER EFFECT:** This is the change in a wave's frequency which depends on how it's moving. The frequency of sound waves coming from a moving fire truck will change depending on whether it's coming towards you or moving away. The pitch will become higher if it's coming towards you (because the sound waves squash together) and lower if it's headed away (because the sound waves stretch).

⭐ **EINSTEIN, ALBERT:** Albert Einstein was pretty smart. He worked out that mass bends space and time. The more massive an object, the more that object bends it. Like dropping a bowling ball on a bed will make a dent and if you roll smaller balls past it, they will curve around the bowling ball.

⭐ **ELECTROMAGNETIC SPECTRUM:** The different wavelengths of electromagnetic radiations. This includes radio waves, visible light, microwaves, infrared light, ultraviolet light, gamma rays, and x-rays.

⭐ **ENERGY:** The amount of potential we have in order to move or generate heat or do anything.

Energy is like pocket money — you can't do the things you want to do without the right amount. Energy is measured in joules.

⭐ **FIRST LAW OF THERMODYNAMICS:** In the 19th century, scientists were beginning to realise that energy is neither created nor destroyed. Building on this work was a man called Rudolf Clausius. What it means is that when you do something, the energy it took is not lost — it's transferred. For example, kicking a ball might cause the energy to be transferred into the movement of a ball and the heat of the air around it. You'll need another chocolate bar to get more energy back.

⭐ **GALAXY:** A galaxy is a collection of solar systems which are all orbiting around a common centre (often that centre is a black hole).

★ **GAMMA RAYS:** These are what made the Incredible Hulk into the cool super hero he is today. But in the real world they are a type of radiation which is found on the electromagnetic spectrum.

★ **GOLDILOCKS ZONE:** An area in a solar system which isn't too far or too close from the sun for life to exist. The problem with this definition is that we are constantly discovering new places in which life might exist, so this area changes a lot. In our solar system it's usually thought of as where Earth is. Because look at all the life on this planet!

⭐ **GRAVITY:** The force which pulls everything towards everything else. It is why stars and planets are formed. It makes it harder to leave the planet and is what draws me towards the fridge when Mum and Dad are in bed. It's science, Mum. I can't fight it.

⭐ **KELVIN:** Not the boy who used to go to my school but a way of measuring temperature.

⭐ **LIGHT YEAR:** The distance light travels through a vacuum (nothing slowing it down or blocking its way) in a year.

⭐ **MICROWAVES:** Another type of radiation found on the electromagnetic spectrum.

⭐ **OBSERVABLE UNIVERSE:** The amount of the universe we can see. The universe may be much larger but we can only look at the parts where light (as any type of radiation on the electromagnetic spectrum) has been able to reach us. When we look at distant objects in space, we are looking back through time almost to when the Big Bang happened.

⭐ **RADIUS:** The distance between the centre of a circle or ellipse and the edge. The diameter is twice this distance.

⭐ **RED SHIFT:** Go and read the bit about the Doppler Effect. OK, hello again. Red shift is like that but with light. If an object is moving away then it appears redder. And the redder it appears then the more it's moving away. That's because the light waves are stretched, and longer light waves appear as red. If it's moving towards you then they look blue. Angry people are blue in the face as they rush towards you shouting **"GIVE ME MY SWEETS"** but embarrassed people are red in the face as they run away mumbling "I honestly thought those were my sweets".

⭐ **SETI:** A project to scan the skies searching for signs of extra-terrestrial life. It stands for the Search for Extra-Terrestrial Intelligence.

⭐ **SOLAR SYSTEM:** An area of space which is controlled by a star's gravity and energy. Solar systems often contain planets and asteroids which orbit the star.

⭐ **SPEED OF LIGHT:** The speed at which light travels through a vacuum. At **299,792.458 km** per second this is the fastest speed there is.

★ ULTRAVIOLET LIGHT: A portion of the electromagnetic spectrum which we can't see with the naked eye (although some animals can).

★ UNIVERSE: Everything that we know exists is in the universe. It's all the stars and planets which form solar systems and galaxies. And cake.

★ X-RAYS: Part of the electromagnetic spectrum that we can't directly see with our eyes, but which can travel through objects (we can use x-rays to take photographs of bones).

★ ZENO: Zeno was a philosopher in Greece a LONG time ago who asked how a moving object can ever reach its destination if it first has to cover half the distance and then half the remaining distance and then half the remaining distance and so on. In other words, there will always be a half of any remaining part of the distance. If I was to make a film (not the one about me), then it would be called Finding Zeno. And we'd never find him.

★ ACKNOWLEDGEMENTS ★

As with Meet Matilda Rocket Builder, this book has been a team effort — from the dedicated efforts of the UCLan Publishing team to the fizzingly wonderful Heidi.

Once again, I found myself reliant on the wisdom and knowledge of the following people.

To Fenner for giving me so much of his time. If any of the details in this book are wrong, then it's entirely his fault for not making me smarter. For Ruth, whose early eyes and enthusiasm helped me keep on going. For super smart author Stuart Atkinson for being patient with me when I was bombarding him with questions about Mars. For Professor James Carter, poet and guiding star. For Commander Amanda, for giving me the idea

to write about how aliens might look and talk.
And for Oliver, so that he will read this book in
the hope of finding himself mentioned.

IF YOU LIKED THIS, YOU'LL LOVE . . .

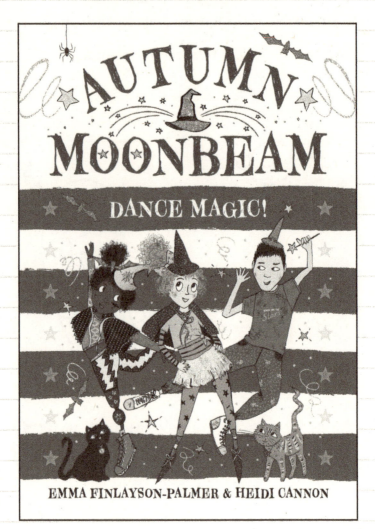

AUTUMN MOONBEAM

DANCE MAGIC!

EMMA FINLAYSON-PALMER & HEIDI CANNON

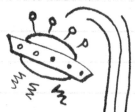

Written by
TASHA HARRISON

CLEMENTINE
FLORENTINE

WHEN YOU'RE IN A FUNK,
YOU NEED POETRY
AND PUNK!

Illustrated by
MYA MITCHELL

THE OCTOPUS,

DADU

AND ME

LUCY ANN UNWIN

Cover Illustration
by SELOM SUNU

Interior Illustrations
by LUCY MULLIGAN

Susan Brownrigg

Gracie
Fairshaw
and the
Mysterious
Guest

Illustrated by Jenny Czerwonka

KICKING OFF!

DICK, KERR GIRLS

EVE AINSWORTH

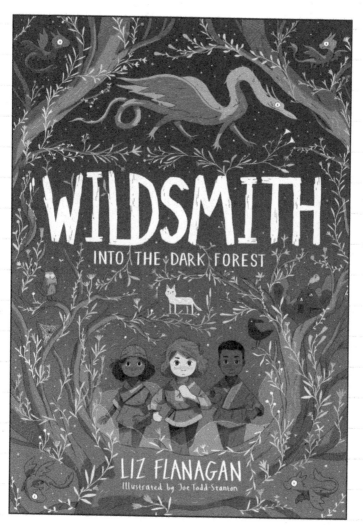

HAVE YOU READ MATILDA'S FIRST ADVENTURE?

MEET MATILDA ROCKET BUILDER

WRITTEN BY **DOM CONLON**

ILLUSTRATED BY **HEIDI CANNON**